A Day in the Life of the Amish

For an inside look at the hard work, pleasant play, hearty meals and devout worship of the "Plain People", we asked 63 Amish families to keep a diary—all on the same day—of their dawn-to-dusk activities.

Publisher: Roy Reiman
Editor: Bob Ottum
Assistant Editors: Joan M. Graff,
Kristine Krueger, Hal Prey
Art Director: Jim Sibilski
Art Assistant: Gail Engeldahl
Photo Coordination: Trudi Bellin
Production Assistants: Ellen Lloyd, Judy Pope

5400 S. 60th St., Greendale WI 53129
International Standard Book Number: 0-89821-126-3
Library of Congress Catalog Card Number: 94-67583

Cover photo by Don Shenk
Page 3 photo by Julie Habel
Back cover photo by Jon Paris
Quilt photos courtesy of The Heritage Center
Museum of Lancaster County, Penn Square,
Lancaster, Pennsylvania

Contents

Amish Settlements

THIS FIRST-EVER MAP in print shows locations (indicated by small black blocks) where Amish have formed communities. Biggest concentration is in Great Lakes states, but some are far west as Montana.

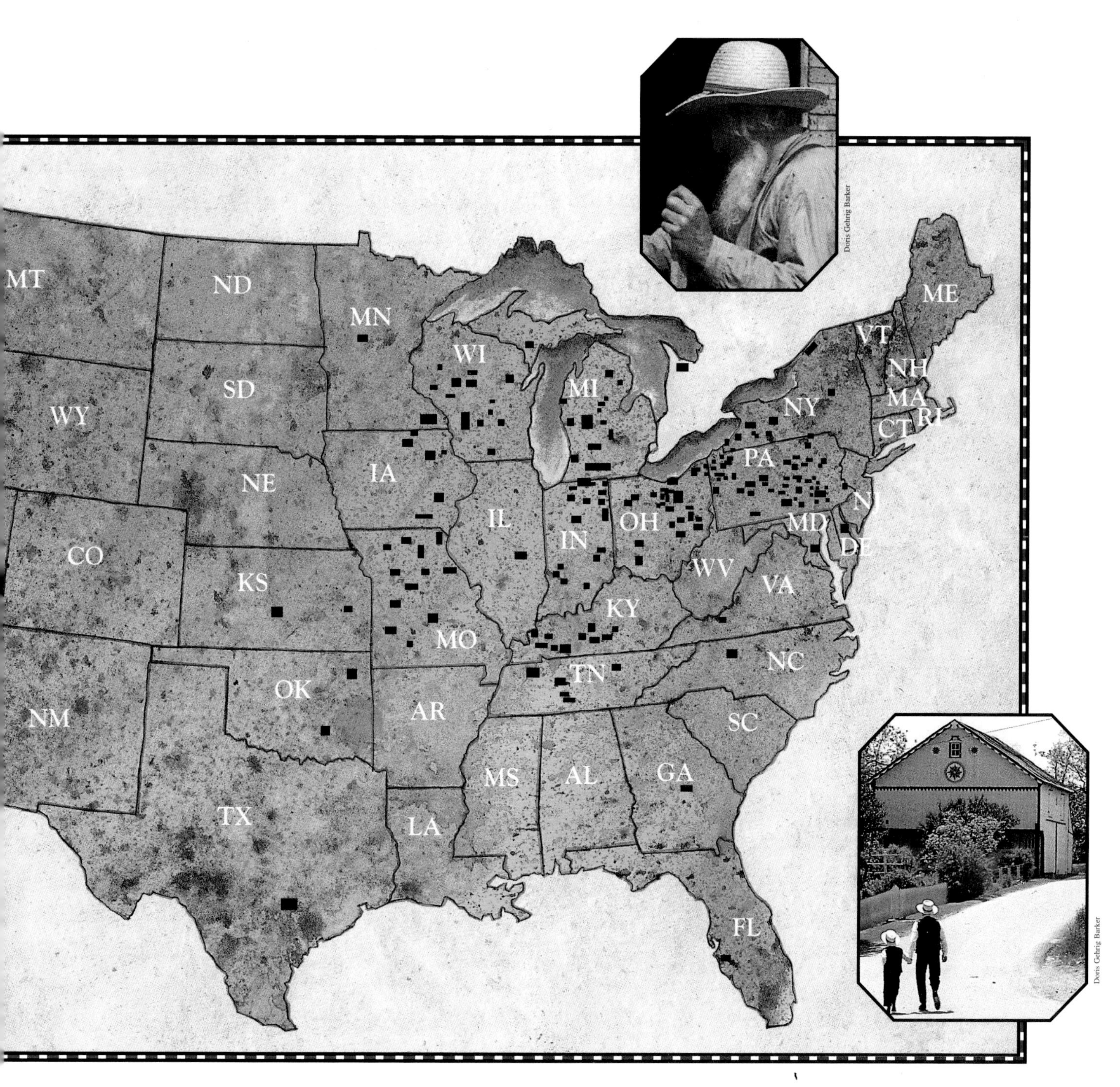

INTRODUCTION

JUST ABOUT everyone is fascinated by the Amish.

Tourists flock to Amish settlements each year to buy handmade furniture, toys and colorful quilts...to sample hearty home-cooked foods...or just to watch "Plain People" at work and play.

That simple, family-centered lifestyle is especially appealing in these fast-paced, high-tech times. Content to let the modern world pass them by, the Amish enjoy a self-reliance and peace of mind many of us long for.

There have been plenty of books *about* the Amish, but not many books *by* the Amish—books that let them describe—*in their own words*—the rewards of hard work, togetherness and rock-solid faith.

A Day in the Life of the Amish is that kind of book, with an interesting twist—most of the photos were taken by the Amish themselves! Along with their diary accounts of a *single day* (Monday, Oct. 4, 1993) these photos provide a uniquely personal glimpse into the everyday life of Amish families in several different states and Canada.

Many people believe that Amish live mostly in Lancaster County, Pennsylvania or Holmes County, Ohio. But you'll learn that today there are large Amish settlements in 22 states and one Canadian province.

To help us locate families willing to write diaries and take photos, we contacted the Mennonite Information Center in Berlin, Ohio, which serves as a clearinghouse for information about Amish and Mennonites.

Volunteer worker Verna Schlabach was happy to answer all of our questions about the Amish. But when we asked for a map of the various settlements, she told us there was no such 

IDEA CLICKED. When we asked over 100 Amish families to keep a "diary" on the same day, we also sent this "one-time-use" camera to many of them to take pictures of their homes, horses, buggies, livestock, etc. As a result, they took most of the photos in this book.

thing—at least, not readily available to the public.

"The only map I know of showing where the Amish live is the large one we have here on our office wall," Verna explained. "Over the years, we've regularly marked the locations of new settlements. But to my knowledge, no one has ever published such a map."

We quickly asked Verna if—in return for a donation to the Center—someone there would be willing to transfer all that information to a smaller map for us. They eagerly said yes.

Amish on the Move?

Verna and an Amish co-worker went a big step further—they painstakingly highlighted every county containing Amish settlements on a state-by-state basis in a large U.S. atlas. We used that atlas to create the map on the previous page—the most complete map of Amish settlements ever published.

In addition to providing the map, Verna answered our questions about why the Amish live where they do, and how they choose new settlements.

"No one is certain where the very first Amish settled in America," Verna related. "But the first formal congregation was formed in Berks County, Pennsylvania in 1749. In the years that followed, Amish tended to settle in hilly areas that reminded them of their native Switzerland."

Nowadays there are other considerations, of course, such as the availability and price of good farmland. Amish farms are small compared to most others found in America—they range in size from 60 to 100 acres, which is as much as can be farmed efficiently with horse-drawn equipment.

"These days, most Amish prefer to move onto established farms," Verna noted. "Earlier on, though, the land needed to be cleared, and barns and homes built first."

Young Amish couples buying their first place usually borrow money from their parents or other relatives rather than from a bank or finance company.

When Amish families move, they often rely on a local trucking company (not necessarily a *moving* company) to haul their possessions. Occasionally a cattle truck is used. "When moving a short distance, horse-drawn hay wagons are often used for transportation," Verna explained.

Finding Amish families to write diaries and take photos for this book was an interesting challenge.

Names and addresses for many potential contributors were provided by the Mennonite Information Center and by publishers of *The Budget*, an Amish newspaper. More were gleaned from among Amish subscribers to Reiman Publications' magazines and from lists of Amish families who host tour groups through Reiman's Country Tours division.

Finally, a letter explaining this project was mailed to more than 100 Amish families, along with a questionnaire and a return envelope. Happily, many families readily agreed to participate. Those who indicated they were willing to take photos were also sent a small "disposable" camera.

"Diary day" was Monday, Oct. 4, 1993. It dawned bright and clear in much of the country; rainy and chilly in some areas. Our Amish correspondents began jotting down details of their activities and snapping photos of their homes, farms, shops and animals.

Several days later, the first of the diaries arrived in the mail at our offices. They were *fascinating*, filled with activities, personal observations and gentle good humor.

Then the cameras began arriving, too (we said we'd develop the film—just send the camera back).

Again, we were delighted with the results! The colorful snapshots were rich with details often overlooked by professional photographers—details that made us feel as if we were right *there* with those Amish families.

Now it's *your* turn to spend a day with friendly Amish folks across the U.S. and Canada. So leave the hectic, harried modern world behind for a few hours and take a buggy ride in the slow lane. We know you'll enjoy it!

—Bob Ottum, Editor

A Word About the Photos...

WHENEVER possible, photos taken by the diarist were used to illustrate his or her diary. If the diarist did not provide photos, those taken by other diarists and showing similar subjects were used to portray the settings.

CHAPTER ONE

Pieced quilt, cotton, made by Barbara Snyder Stoner of
West Earl Township, Lancaster County, c. 1885-1900.

Carol Duerkson

MONDAY is wash day in most Amish households. At the Haven, Kansas farmhouse of Clayton and Ann Knepp, church clothes and work clothes fill up the clothesline—and the porch.

Chicken and Noodles Are on Menu in Ohio

◆ PROFILE ◆

On their farm near Sugarcreek, Lester and Ruby Beachy raise broilers on contract for Case Farms of Ohio, and make and sell homemade noodles—nearly a ton a week! The Beachys have four daughters: Hannah, 10, Sharon, 8, Rhoda, 6, and Regina, 3-1/2. Lester kept this diary.

Welcome, everyone, to "Limpytown", here in the beautiful rolling hills of eastern Holmes County.

Limpytown really is not a town at all—it is just a crossroad out in the country away from the crowds of tourists that come flocking to Holmes County each year to try to get a taste of the simple life and sense of belonging that society seems to have lost. In years gone by, a man with a wooden leg used to live in this area—hence the name Limpytown.

The alarm clock had us rolling out of bed at 6 o'clock this morning. After breakfast I went outside to check on our broilers while Ruby got the girls up and helped them with breakfast and packing their lunch.

By the time our three workers arrived, I was ready to begin with our homemade noodles. We make about a ton of noodles a week; they're mostly sold wholesale.

Our girls used to attend public school until this year, when the potential for harm in the public school system motivated our church to build our own school. The girls really like their new school. It is a two-room schoolhouse with a capacity for 66 students.

Every Monday, the brethren of our church take turns to have a short Bible reading with the pupils. It was my turn today, so after getting Ruby and the workers started on the noodles, I hitched our horse to the buggy and headed for school, accompanied by 3-1/2-year-old Regina. With the other three in school, she usually gets to go with Daddy.

I arrived home in good time to help with the noodles yet. We were finished by noontime, and Ruby started washing. Monday is usually a wash day, as the Sunday clothes need to be washed.

KNOWN FOR NOODLES. Tasty sideline keeps family members busy. Noodles (shown drying on racks) are sold wholesale.

We had attended Sunday School on Sunday—our church has regular services every 2 weeks and Sunday School on the in-between Sundays. Our church is right now in the process of dividing into two congregations. We have our services in our homes, and when the church becomes too large, this necessitates that either some relocate or the congregation divides.

We all sat down to a delicious supper of chicken and our homemade noodles. Suppertime is a time of sharing the day's events with each other. A beautiful sunset in the evening held promise of another nice day tomorrow.

BY THE TIME I had the dinner dishes cleared away, the iceman came. He has a regular route on Mondays and Thursdays to deliver ice during the warm months. In only a few more weeks, his job will be finished for another season.

He has refrigeration on his truck and carries 10- and 25-pound blocks of ice and also 10-pound bags of ice cubes. He also carries soft drinks and ice cream, and during the summer months when the schoolchildren have vacation, his air horn brings them running, which he enjoys.

Today we got only one 25-pound block as we usually do on Mondays. We get two on Thursdays—with that schedule, we never run out of ice.

We have a homemade icebox in which we place the ice in the top compartment. The food is kept in the lower compartment, which is cooled from the ice above. As the ice melts, the water runs down a drain hose to the basement drain below.

—Mary Miller
Punxsutawney, Pennsylvania

BUGGY "GARAGE" is located in lower level of Beachys' barn, built on slope.

Grandchildren a Blessing to Busy Widow

◆ PROFILE ◆

Effie Troyer, 81, has been a widow for nearly 6 years. She and her husband raised eight children on the family farm near Dover; now Effie has 64 grandchildren and 9 great-grandchildren. Effie's oldest son and his family work the farm, growing mostly alfalfa and corn. They have four workhorses and 17 milk cows.

Walter Tro

This chilly morning I started a fire in both stoves, kitchen and living room, for the first time this fall, but let it go out later as daughter Mary and her daughter Linda came to help me turn a basket of yellow Delicious apples into sauce.

We used the oil stove and camp stove to cook and can the apples. Mary brought me a big serving of pretzel salad which they had yesterday for their dinner (though I do believe, instead of pretzels, she used graham crackers to make it). They went home before dinnertime, as Linda wanted to go help pot mums at a local greenhouse where they raise thousands of them.

Today would be the last day she would be helping there as she plans to leave by Amtrak with her friend, first to Indiana to meet his parents, then to Middlefield, Ohio, to attend the wedding of his brother on October 14, and home again to attend the wedding of her brother on October 21.

"My old feet don't take being on them so much."

After they left, I tried to rest, as my old feet don't take being on them so much anymore.

Daughter-in-law Matilda and Rhoda, 20, did a big wash, some ironing and mending some of the boys' pants, which Matilda said were ripped from A to Z.

Matilda also cleaned a one-burner oil stove, which is to be used on October 23 to cook raised doughnuts at the large consignment sale for benefit of our parochial schools.

Marvin, almost 15, cleaned the barnyard and also hauled shavings into the henhouse, which I think the new pullets appreciated. Freddie, 18, was working at his uncle's sawmill, which is his regular job. Roy, 19, mowed some late hay.

Corn is on shock, and gardens are

❖ Who Are the Amish and Why That Name? ❖

WE READ and hear the name "Amish" quite often these days. Tourists drive hundreds of miles to see Amish country and visit Amish stores and shops. Many businesses use the name to advertise and sell their food and merchandise, adding the word "Amish" to goods that never were close to an Amish person at all.

Although there are *some* Amish people who use the name to sell their merchandise, there are hundreds or perhaps thousands of our people who wish the name would not be used in such a way. Our food and our merchandise are not better than that of many others in this world, and this flattery is not good for any Christian.

Here is a brief history of the Amish: In the 1500's, in the Netherlands, a young Catholic priest named Menno Simons was dissatisfied with the unchristian morals and non-scriptured teachings of the Catholic church.

While reading the Bible and studying its teachings, he was driven to his knees in earnest prayer, asking for wisdom and direction from God. He was rewarded with spiritual power and a regenerated heart to help others see the Gospel way and ended up preaching God's Word.

Before long, Menno's followers were being called "Mennonites". After a life full of preaching, Menno died in his 66th year in 1561 A.D.

The Mennonite movement grew for many years, but by 1700, there was strife and disagreement in the Mennonite church. It ended in a division led by Jacob Ammon, who broke away to start a more conservative church.

This new group of followers was called "Amish" after their leader. Hence the Amish had their roots in the Mennonite church after breaking away from the Catholic church.

—Levi L. Hershberger, Guys Mills, Pennsylvania

Amos Eicher

David Yutzy

ONE-ROOM SCHOOLS like the one opposite are where most Amish youngsters are educated. Diarist Esther Borntranger teaches 30 pupils, grades one through eight, all together in a classroom like the one above. Right: Large gardens provide plenty of potatoes, squash and corn for families.

empty except for squash and some tomatoes yet.

Soon the other grandchildren are home from school. Little Nancy, almost 3, has an hour's ride on the bus to a special school for hearing impaired. Elsie, Henry, Freeman and Junior go to school near home, which was the first Amish parochial school in the U.S.A., built in 1925.

Little Ivan, 4 years old, comes to my house asking if I need wood, expecting a treat of a pack of Smarties. He also brings me my mail, which today consists only of two letters pleading for money, all for a good cause, of course.

Son Roman, who owns the farm, was working all day in setting up new milkers. As soon as the boys were home from school, he sent Junior to a neighbor for a plastic pipe.

He got one milker ready to use tonight, so the whole family, including me, was out to see how it works. Matilda did quite a few cows by hand yet tonight.

Yesterday at the end of our church services, announcement was made of the forthcoming weddings of a grandson on October 21 and a granddaughter on October 28. I just recently attended the wedding of another granddaughter in Mondovi, Wisconsin. Now I'm looking forward to more!

Teacher Enjoys Challenge Of 30 Lively Little 'Scholars'

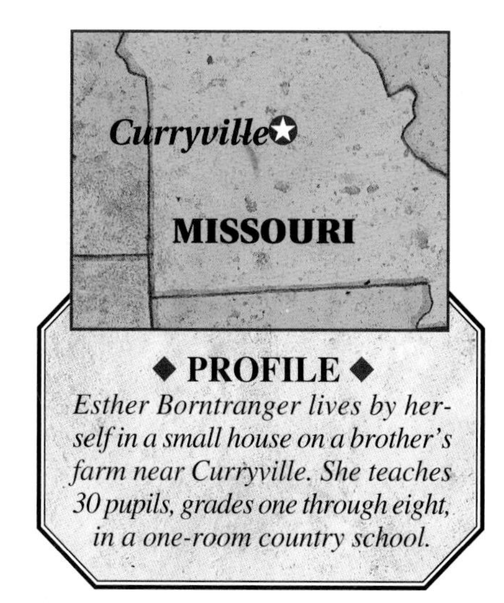

◆ PROFILE ◆

Esther Borntranger lives by herself in a small house on a brother's farm near Curryville. She teaches 30 pupils, grades one through eight, in a one-room country school.

I got up at 6 a.m. as usual, ate a hurried breakfast, packed a lunch of a sandwich, cookies and a thermos of coffee, then was on my way to another day at school.

The 1/4-mile walk sure didn't seem far on such a beautiful day! The sky was clear blue and cloudless, the temperature was in the upper 50's and the leaves were changing color, truly a wonderful sight.

We started our day at 9 with prayer and song. Then I spent about 15 minutes with first graders, who are learning the letter sounds and doing real well with them. I'm also teaching them the names of the basic colors.

The other classes did their reading lessons. My helper, Katie Schwartz, stayed busy checking homework and answering questions.

At 10:45, we turned to our arithmetic workbooks. Katie watched over the first graders and helped them when they needed help while I continued with arithmetic classes.

At 12 we dismissed for lunch. The pupils all ate their lunches outside, sitting on the grass. One of the third grade girls brought me a big piece of pie. At 12:45, I rang the bell again, and after everyone had gotten their drinks at the pump and were in their seats, I read them a chapter from the book *Four Little Mischiefs*. They just love story time!

I worked with first grade awhile again while the others had oral spelling. The fifth grade had a hard time with the word "question", and most of them missed it. Katie checked workbooks between answering raised hands and helping some of the pupils with more math problems.

At 2 we dismissed for a 15-minute recess, which stretched into 25 since it was such a beautiful day. A neighbor had hired a dozer who was working in the field beside the playground, and

Levi Burkholder

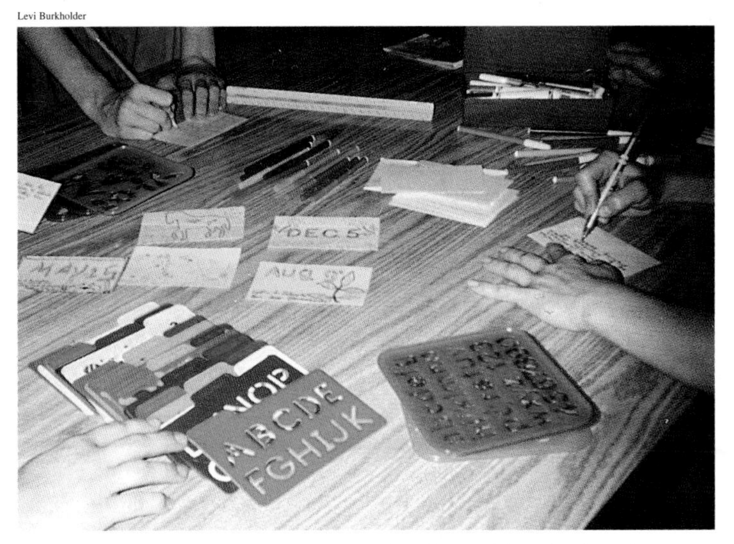

THE A-B-C'S of education are emphasized in Amish schools, where students concentrate on basic skills. Older pupils help their younger classmates.

the pupils were very interested in watching.

At 2:25 school was again in session. I gave the first graders their workbooks to do, which involved cutting and pasting, something they enjoy as much as coloring.

When they color animals, I tell them to color them as they are, not blue or green. Once one little boy colored a dog blue, so I asked him if he ever saw a blue dog. He looked at me in all innocence and replied, "Yes, our blue heeler!" That made my day.

The third graders had phonics workbooks to do, and the rest had geography or social studies. Before we dismissed at 3:30, two of the girls swept the floor and another washed the boards. After the students left, Katie and I finished up our work, closed the shutters and left for home.

When I arrived home, I was greeted by a lively bundle of sunshine in the form of my tiny house dog named, of course, "Sunshine". She gets quite lonely being by herself every day and is overjoyed when I come home at night.

Later tonight, brother Henry and his two children, Verena and Nathaniel, came by with horse and buggy, so Sunshine and I got a ride with them to Dad and Mom's for a supper of apple dumplings, dressing and canned chicken bologna.

We called it a night at 9:30. 

Garden Season's Short Way Out West

◆ PROFILE ◆

After 22 years in Bloomfield, Iowa, David and Ella Yutzy recently moved to an Amish settlement of 15 families in northwestern Montana near Rexford, just 2 miles from the Canadian border. With son Gideon, 23, and daughter Esther, 19, they run a harness shop, grocery and craft store. David kept this diary.

At 6:30 this morning the moon was shining brightly, but soon a heavy fog moved in from Lake Koocanusa, which is 2 miles away. This happens almost every morning at this time of year, but usually by forenoon the fog clears out and the rest of the day is clear.

Our settlement is the farthest north and west in America, started in 1975. The nearest town is Eureka, 30 miles southeast. Our post office is at Rexford, a little village on the east side of Lake Koocanusa.

Lake Koocanusa was formed in 1972 after the Libby Dam was built across the Kootenai River. A mile wide and 90 miles long, half of the lake is in Canada and the other half in the U.S.

There are 15 Amish families living around here, but this amount varies from time to time. Last winter there were only eight. The largest amount ever was 23 families. Presently 11 Amish students are enrolled in a log cabin schoolhouse just across the road from our home.

> **"Around here, you need a tall fence to keep deer out of the garden!"**

Our 4-bedroom log home is nestled on 6-1/2 acres among dark green pines. The home, now 6 years old, was put up by Kootenai Log Homes, a business which adjoins our backyard. The business is owned by six young Amish men and employs about 12 boys and girls.

At present, they are starting to cut logs for a 2,000-square-foot home, the largest one for this year, to be built in Missoula, Montana. Our son Gideon works on the road crew and goes all over to put up these log homes. He's in Denver, Colorado, right now.

One-half mile northeast of us is Border Lumber Company, where 20-plus men and boys are employed. It is owned by Wayne Door Co. of Ohio, and managed by Ivan Miller.

Another occupation of the Amish here is raising beef cattle and growing alfalfa hay. John Miller, one of the first settlers of this area, raises registered Arabian horses, which he is getting ready for a production sale this coming spring.

It didn't take me long to do my morning chores, if you call feeding a few chickens chores! Next I got out the tiller and finished tilling our garden for next spring. The soil is very fine and loose.

We had a very good garden this year, but because of the short growing season, a few things such as sweet corn barely made it before the first frost. There is a 7-foot-high rail fence around our garden. Around here, you need a tall fence to keep the deer out!

For breakfast we had whole-wheat

LOTS OF LOGS. Logging and building log homes are main industries in farthest-west Amish settlement. Yutzy family runs grocery store and craft shop near their cozy log home (center).

biscuits and hamburger gravy, orange juice, fresh garden tea and my favorite cereal, homemade grapenuts, made by my wife in the store bakery. We took over managing Kootenai Kraft and Groceries when we moved out here.

The store is about 30 rods down the road. The clerks are daughter Esther and my niece Ruby Yutzy. They change off, so today Esther was doing our weekly laundry.

Besides a full line of groceries, we sell some hardware, quilts, rugs and other crafts. We also sell feed, gas, kerosene and propane and run a locker service, renting out freezer compartments. The store is open from 9 a.m. to 6 p.m., with free coffee all day!

Ella was busy this morning packing suitcases and making preparations for our trip back East to visit family. We'll leave from Whitefish, Montana on Amtrak Wednesday morning. Our first stop will be in Wisconsin to visit our sons, then on to Iowa to visit the rest of the family. I am looking forward to seeing our 36 grandchildren!

For lunch I had an apple and a banana out of the store and more tea, as I'm trying to lose a little weight.

In the afternoon I worked in our harness and tack shop, which is on the hill behind our house, open 1 to 6 p.m. Standing at my harness stitcher sewing, I have a good view of the beautiful Rocky Mountains north and east of us up in Canada.

To the west of us we have a good view of Mount Robinson. Some hikers going up last week got a close look at a mountain lion. Other wildlife commonly sighted in our area includes black bear, elk, moose, white-tail and mule deer, mountain goats and sheep, wild turkeys and grouse. At night we often hear coyotes yapping in the distance.

We get lots of out-of-state hunters and lots of other tourists during the summer. Some people say we have only three seasons—tourist, hunting and winter!

Supper was served tonight at 6:30 and included fried chicken, escalloped potatoes, baked beans, carrots and celery. Afterward, we took ice cream and a birthday cake over to our good friends, the Allen Bontragers. Allen's wife Arlene had a birthday today. Our neighbor, Chris Yoder, also stopped in to visit for awhile.

We arrived home after a refreshing walk in the crisp night air. I still had some reading to do, including the four letters from Iowa we got in today's mail. By the time I got that done, it was 11 and time to hit the hay.

Amish Barn Raising...

From Bare to Barn In Under 6 Hours!

THE AMISH are well-known for their willingness to help one another out in difficult times, and there's no better example of this than an old-fashioned barn raising.

When lightning struck Wayne Burkholder's barn near Farmerstown, Ohio, it burned down in a hurry. Two weeks later, when 700 members of his community came to help, a brand-new barn went up in a hurry, too.

The men began arriving in their buggies right after breakfast, and the roof was on the barn when they broke for lunch!

Photographer Doyle Yoder was on hand throughout the day to document the event in these dramatic photos.

As you study the pictures, think of the organization this project required with hundreds of workers...imagine the sound of the hammering and shouts as the structure developed...and think how hungry these men must have been for the huge picnic lunch served by the women at noon!

1. End walls go up first as work begins in early morning. Portable sawmill is usually set up on the farm and lumber is cut from timber a few days before raising.

HILLSIDE FANS. Amish wives and children pause to watch barn take shape, then begin preparing lunch. Many came from long distances in buggies.

Photos by Doyle Yoder

2. Workers use long poles (photo at left) to hoist frames, then men at top nail them in place. Some frames are done day before and laid on floor.

3. At noon, men line up (upper right) to wash before lunch, then join another line (at right) for buffet of Amish cooking, including side dishes, homemade bread and desserts that the women brought in their buggies. Note all the straw hats on lawn and even on the roof of the shed.

4. Photo below was taken just prior to lunch, and shows last sheets of roofing and last of siding being applied. With stalls and concrete block walls prepared by several "advance" carpenters a few days before, farm owner Wayne Burkholder was able to move in cows same night.

Cooking, Quilting Fill Busy Days on Iowa Family Farm

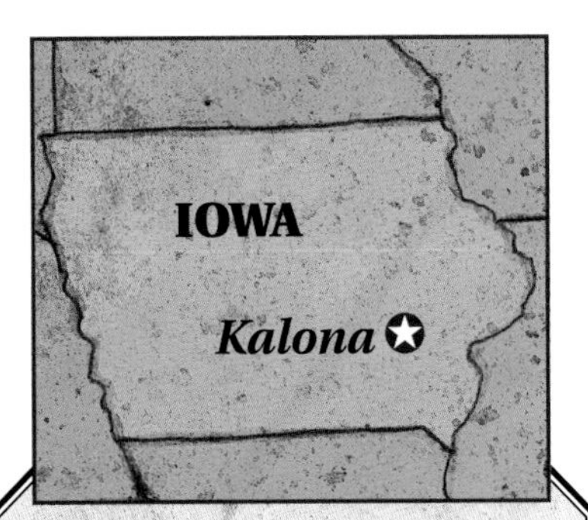

◆ PROFILE ◆

Mary Ellen Gingerich and her brother Emil live on their farm near Kalona in Johnson County with a grandniece and her husband, who does the farming. Mary Ellen takes care of house and garden and likes to quilt for a hobby. Her brother helps with the farm where needed and is also treasurer of their school and helps order books, does payroll and utilities.

Andrew Yoder

Amos Eicher

David Miller

Jonas Coblentz

"PUTTING BY" apples and a variety of vegetables from large gardens keeps Amish women especially busy during summer and fall. Lack of modern kitchen appliances doesn't prevent them from stocking pantry and basement shelves with hundreds of jars of food for the winter.

The alarm goes off at 5:30. Even though I'm retired, I still like to get up early, so I jump out of bed. With a quick look at the indoor-outdoor thermometer, I note the temperature is at 50°, so a fire is made in the kitchen range, and it feels real good!

Today is wash day. As we are still old-fashioned and cannot just open the faucet and let hot water out for washing, I go to the washhouse to pump water into the iron kettle. I must not forget to take water along for priming the pump, as it usually is drained.

"We cannot just open the faucet for hot water..."

I know exactly how much water it will take for the washing, as I have often counted the strokes, and after having pumped 230 times, I know the kettle is now full enough. The wood and cobs had been put into the washhouse on Saturday eve, so they are ready to start the fire.

Back to the house to get the breakfast ready. This morning I decide to have hominy. It had been made this summer and canned in jars. Hominy along with eggs and apple sauce make up our meal, along with cereal and fruit on top.

Next come morning devotions, singing a hymn, reading a chapter from the Bible and having prayer.

After dishes are washed, the water for washing is hot, so the wash is sorted. The belt from the line shaft is put on the double-tub Dexter washing machine, the Honda motor is started and the washing begins.

By 10 o'clock, the wash is on the line and fluttering in the nice breeze on this sunshiny day. Next, the "Double Wedding Ring" quilt that was taken out of frame on Saturday is trimmed in preparation for putting binding on it whenever a convenient time arises.

Dinnertime approaches, so I go out to the garden to see what goodies are there yet. I find some lima beans that are ready, so they are quickly picked and shelled, washed and put on the stove to cook.

Our meal consists of creamed potatoes, buttered lima beans, sausage balls from a jar out of the basement, pumpkin pudding and for dessert some of our own home-raised white peaches and pumpkin bars.

The wash dries till after the dinner dishes are done, then the ironing is done as well as the patching.

Around 3:30, I take time to make a trip to Iowa City to the chiropractor, to try to get relief for my aching back. As it is rather late when I come home, I make a hurried supper of chicken noodle soup along with minced ham sandwiches, cheese, Chinese cabbage with peanut butter, fruit and bars.

After supper, the "Merry Mary" circle letter, which arrived in the day's mail, is read and enjoyed, and then a sheet is written to include in its send-off.

By then, it is 9:30 and time for bed. Good night!

DURING the day, my thoughts went to the sermons in church yesterday, and how it was brought out that there is nothing of more value than "the peace of God, which passeth all understanding." How true!

I also had to think we can keep records of what happens every day, and if we decide to omit something, we can, but there is One who keeps a record of our entire life.

We are so thankful for the gift of salvation and the freedom of worship we have in our country.

—Fannie Miller, Sears, Michigan

Couple Finds Diversity's Delicious

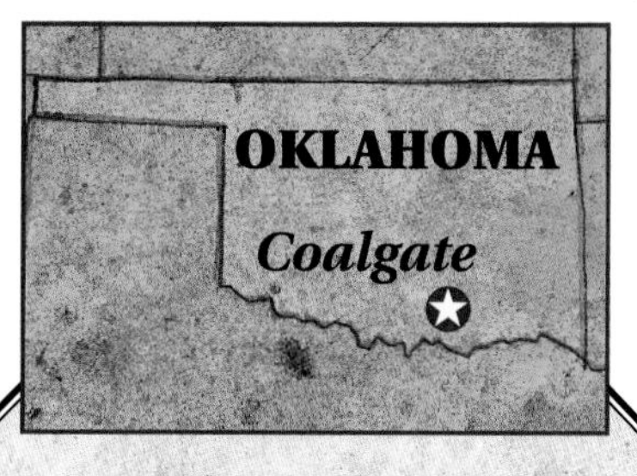

◆ PROFILE ◆

Norman and Sylvia Miller raise cattle on 40 acres of grassland and catfish in two ponds on their farm near Coalgate. In addition they breed a variety of poultry and fowl. Norman works as a carpenter and Sylvia does custom quilting. Sylvia kept this diary.

I was awake and enjoying the bright moonlight when the alarm went off at 6 a.m. We had a quick breakfast of bacon, homemade granola cereal, chocolate revel bars and coffee. After breakfast I packed Norman's lunch while he got his tools together to go to work.

The driver came to get Norman, along with his helper, Herman Joe Stutzman, at 7 o'clock. This morning they started a big roofing job on a church-house in Stonewall. This is probably the biggest roof Norman has ever done. It will take 74 square shingles.

After breakfast dishes were done, I got the clothes together and did my weekly washing. I had an extra big laundry, as I washed the curtains and some rugs. I'm cleaning the house from top to bottom these days since we're having church services in our home next Sunday.

At 9:15 I was back in the house and made myself a cup of coffee. It tasted good after being out in the damp 50° air. Next I did my daily sweeping and getting everything straightened up. There was more to do than usual, as six of our neighbor families came last night with cake and ice cream to remind me that I'm a year older. (My birthday was last week.) I got the dishes, tables and chairs back in place, then finished cleaning out the last of the kitchen cabinets.

This afternoon I finished quilting a pillow sham to match a "Flying Geese" quilt I custom quilted for a lady from Coalgate. Before long the laundry was dry, so I brought it in and put it all away and even got the ironing done.

Eldon Rapp

POULTRY flocks provide eggs, meat and also extra income for many Amish families.

At 5 p.m. it was chore time. Our white American Eskimo dog, "Barney", greeted me as I went out to feed and water the diamond doves, ring doves and silver pheasants.

"Andy", our dun Arabian quarter horse, greeted me hungrily at his feed trough, where I gave him oats.

The Belted Galloways and Brangus Heifers were next to be fed. Last were the Silkie and Selright chickens, the Blue Gazzi Modenas and the White King pigeons.

Norman came home at 6 o'clock and we had huntington chicken casserole for supper.

Later, Norman hitched up Andy and took a buggy wheel that needed fixing to the neighbors. I walked down to the pond and fed the fish. On the way I marveled at the wildflowers, the goldenrod, broomweed, the purple button snake-root...how brilliant they all are this fall!

As the sun was going down, my mind went to Psalm 113:3, *From the rising of the sun to the place where it sets—the name of the Lord is to be praised.*

Norman was coming home as I walked into the yard, and a car drove in just ahead of him. It was Monroe and Naomi Yoder, our cousins from Blountstown, Florida. They will be staying with us for a few days.

Just before we went to bed at 9:30, I made the bed in the basement for our guests. As the lights went out, I thanked the Lord for another rewarding day.

They Have Lots of Chairs But No Time for Sitting

◆ PROFILE ◆

Paul and Lena Helmuth operate a woodworking shop where they build and repair furniture and refinish antiques. A neighbor, Ike Swarey, works their 40-acre farm for them. The Helmuths have one daughter, Virginia, 12. Lena kept this diary.

THE DRIVER'S SEAT. After helping daughter Virginia get ready for a ride behind "Star" (top), Paul and Lena get started on the day's chores, which include several loads of laundry (above), harvesting squash (opposite bottom) and building chairs in workshop (opposite top).

IT WAS a chilly 32° this morning with very clear skies.

We did not get up as early as we wanted to, being so tired from our weekend trip to Worthington, Indiana, which is southwest of Indianapolis.

The three of us had gone with our youth group Friday noon and spent Saturday in a state park. Attended church services there with the Amish group on Sunday, and also the hymn singing Sunday evening.

First thing this morning, Paul went out to the barn and fed our two driving horses, "Flame" and "Lady", and Virginia's pony, "Star". While Virginia was getting dressed for school, I packed her lunch.

After Paul came in, we had our usual breakfast of cold cereal (unusual for an Amish family, but that's what we prefer).

Following family devotions, Virginia headed for school on her bicycle. She has only half a mile to go. Paul went over to chat with our neighbor, Ike Swarey. Ike and Paul are both Belgian horse lovers. Ike farms with Belgians, and his stud is from the Doc Newman breeding out of Iowa.

With the beautiful morning and the big pile of dirty wash, I decided to do the laundry before going to help Paul in the shop. He's making a new drop-leaf table that will extend to 9 feet when opened, plus 4 matching chairs.

Sarah Jane Jones, a neighbor girl who helps in the shop, came to work this morning, so the rest of the morning we helped varnish chairs that we are refinishing.

Paul is a contact person for M.D.S. (Mennonite Disaster Service) for our area. We received a letter in the mail

OUR HORSE is named "Trix", and she has the right name, I think, as she can open her box stall door if we don't have an extra snap hooked on.

Our dog, "Pepper", is an Australian blue heeler and is tied near the barn. If Trix gets out of the pasture in any way, Pepper will bark until we go and put her in again. He's let us know a couple of times at night already that the horse was in the yard. He'll bark and bark until we come out.

Pepper also likes to pretend his water dish is a basketball. The children have their basketball net nearby, and when he sees them play, the next thing he's throwing his dish in the air, too! *—Effie Troyer, Mt. Hope, Ohio*

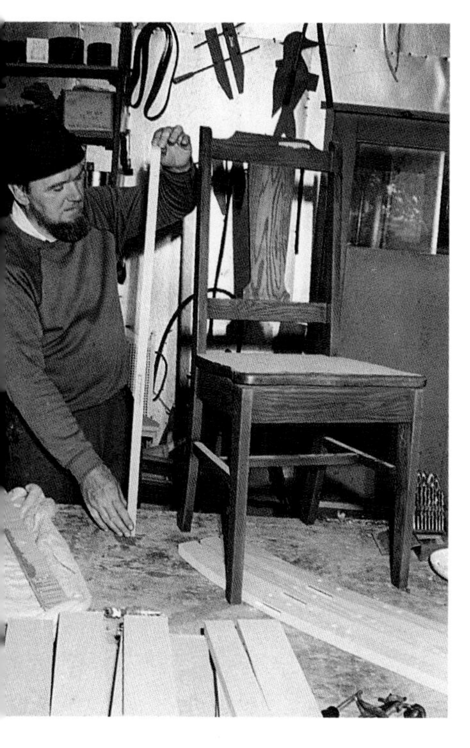

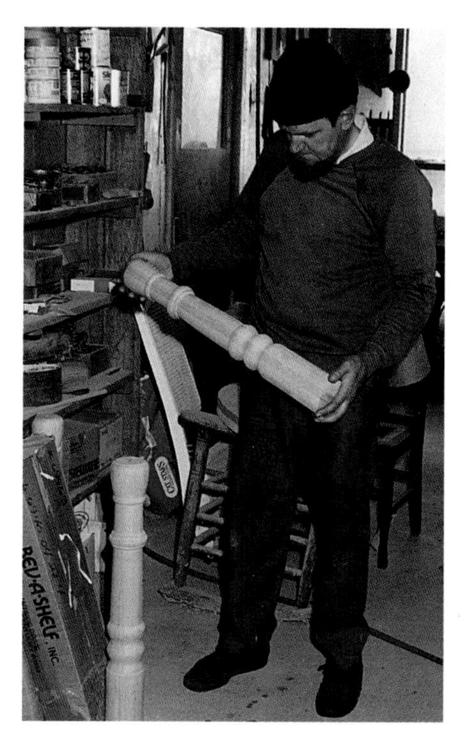

from M.D.S., pleading for help in the Midwest flood area. Last fall, two vanloads from our church went to Franklin, Louisiana to help on the Hurricane Andrew project.

After a lunch of grilled cheese sandwiches and sliced tomatoes from our garden, Paul and I headed for our school for a little fun playing volleyball with the teacher and the pupils. I found again that I'm no spring chicken anymore!

When we came back home, Paul worked on sanding more chairs. The chairs we make have 15 parts, and we sand them all before assembling them. This afternoon we also stained a table and four chairs plus refinished a child's rocker.

Virginia came home from school and, after a snack, hitched up Star to the cart and gave him his afternoon exercise. After that, she mowed some lawn, but did not get very far, as it was time to bring in the wash from the wash line.

For supper we had rib eye steak, cheese potatoes, lima beans and fried green tomatoes. Then it was time to get to the school board meeting, which is only a hop, skip and a jump away.

One of the parents brought a wagonload of slab wood to the school to burn this winter, so the men unloaded that until it was time to start the meeting.

On the way home, we stopped at the neighbor's to get 2 gallons of milk from their bulk tank. Before going to bed, we each had a dish of ice cream. After devotions, we said good night.

AS I WAS harnessing the horses, neighbor Dan Yoder drove in the lane with a hay mower. After a short chat, he was off to our hayfield back yonder to cut the last of our third of cutting hay. We won't be needing it with our cows gone, so I told him he could have it if he makes it.

When Clara came in from hanging the wash, what a sight she found. Little Linda Sue and Barbara Ann had unrolled a whole roll of toilet paper to do some imaginary cleaning on their baby dolls, as they claimed they were so messy! Such is life for the farmer and his wife.

—Eli Weaver, Dundee, Ohio

Beautiful Surroundings Truly Priceless

◆ PROFILE ◆

Andy and Emma Weaver grow greenhouse plants plus corn, oats and hay to feed heifers bred in partnership with son Ben. Andy also works as a self-employed carpenter/painter. The Weavers have seven children: Ben, 25, Rebecca, 19, Elizabeth, 18, Mary, 15, Andrew, 11, Melvin, 9, and Emma, 7. Also considered part of the family is "Judy", their 23-yr-old buggy horse. Emma kept this diary.

Seemed impossible it was time to get up already when the alarm went off around 4. As Andy is working on a construction job, we have to get up extra early. He leaves soon after 5.

The men did the chores. I had thought we'd still be working at silo-filling today, but they finished it on Saturday. Now Ben will go to work with Andy again for several weeks, as he does through slack times.

For breakfast we had home-canned sliced bacon, eggs, toast, fruit and cereal and sweet rolls. While I made breakfast, the girls packed lunches, and Rebecca and Mary got ready for their jobs teaching school. Rebecca teaches grades 1, 2, 6, 7, 8, and Mary 3, 4, 5. They left soon after the men did.

After the first morning rush, Elizabeth and I had a little time to catch our breath. I finished writing a letter, and she got the fire going under the big kettle in the washhouse where we do laundry.

The scholars got up and ready for school and left at 6:50 on the public school bus. (Once the buses all get in at Jasper School, the Amish children get on one bus and are taken to Maple Grove Parochial. It's nice that the Amish children are taken to school this way. After all, we DO pay school taxes!)

I had to put in a new wick on one of the oil stove burners and fill the reservoir on the wood stove. It sits on the back of the stove and is also the shelf for the stove. This reservoir provides us with plenty of hot water.

Since it was sunny and not so cold, I decided to work in the flower garden. We had flowers on three sides of the greenhouse this year for my cut-flower business.

I dug up the gladiola bulbs and cut off the tops. Can't remember bulbs having such long roots other years. Were they reaching down for moisture? Then I gathered seeds from other flowers and pulled out some plants.

Hardly any flowers left, so I decided I'd better get what's there and cut what will likely be our last bouquet except for the pansies. They'll bloom until covered with snow.

Back indoors, it only took 5 minutes to churn the cream to butter. Then I quilted on a Lone Star quilt we're doing. We'll try and sell it at the local quilt shop.

Yesterday church services were at my brother Melvin's place. Announcement was made of the forthcoming marriage of their daughter Martha and Emanuel E. Mullet. We are hoping to see quite a few of my sisters and brothers at the wedding.

There were 11 girls and 4 boys in our family (one sister has passed away), so there is quite a gang of us, and heaps of fun when we get together!

We stayed until dark, and "Judy" was quite eager to head for home. It was hard to believe she's 23, the way she pulled on the lines and trotted.

When I went to the garden to get some goodies for supper, I took time to look around and enjoy the fall splendor.

We are surrounded by hills; some are wooded, some have fields, and at this time of year, they are simply awesome! Recent rains have greened up the fields, and with the multi-colored trees in the background, plus the blue, blue skies, it truly is a sight to behold. If we'd have to pay to view all this beauty, we'd never be able to afford it!

While Andrew and Melvin did the evening chores, Rebecca filled the wood box and filled the oil lamps, and Mary worked at pulling out plants in the flower garden. Emma helped me gather veggies and wash the carrots.

For supper we had mashed potatoes, canned meat loaf, buttered carrots and broccoli with cheese. For dessert, I made apple crisp.

Getting up early means going to bed early, so everyone was in bed soon after 8 p.m.

It is very unusual if nothing unexpected happens here every day—people dropping in, etc. I guess the unexpected today was that nothing unexpected happened!

FLOYD SAYS if there's still daylight when he gets home from his job at the trailer factory, he's gonna go hunting for our wild hog.

Last year about this time, a sow got out, unknown to us, and pigged in our neighbor's cornfield. When they went to fill their silo, they spotted her. That was usually all we saw of her—just a glimpse. As her pigs got older, she became a little less wild, so that we could get close enough to identify her as ours by the ear tag.

Trying to chase her home was a big problem. Didn't work too good to entice her with feed—she had all the corn and water she wanted. We eventually got her in after lots of unsuccessful tries. Several weeks later, we got 9 of the 10 pigs. Now one is still on the loose.

Son Karl had just recently seen some fresh tracks of it. Floyd and several of the boys went hunting in hopes of getting it...guess they are hungry for some fresh pork chops. They came home an hour later and hadn't even seen it. *—Laureen Miller, Milford, Indiana*

CHAPTER TWO

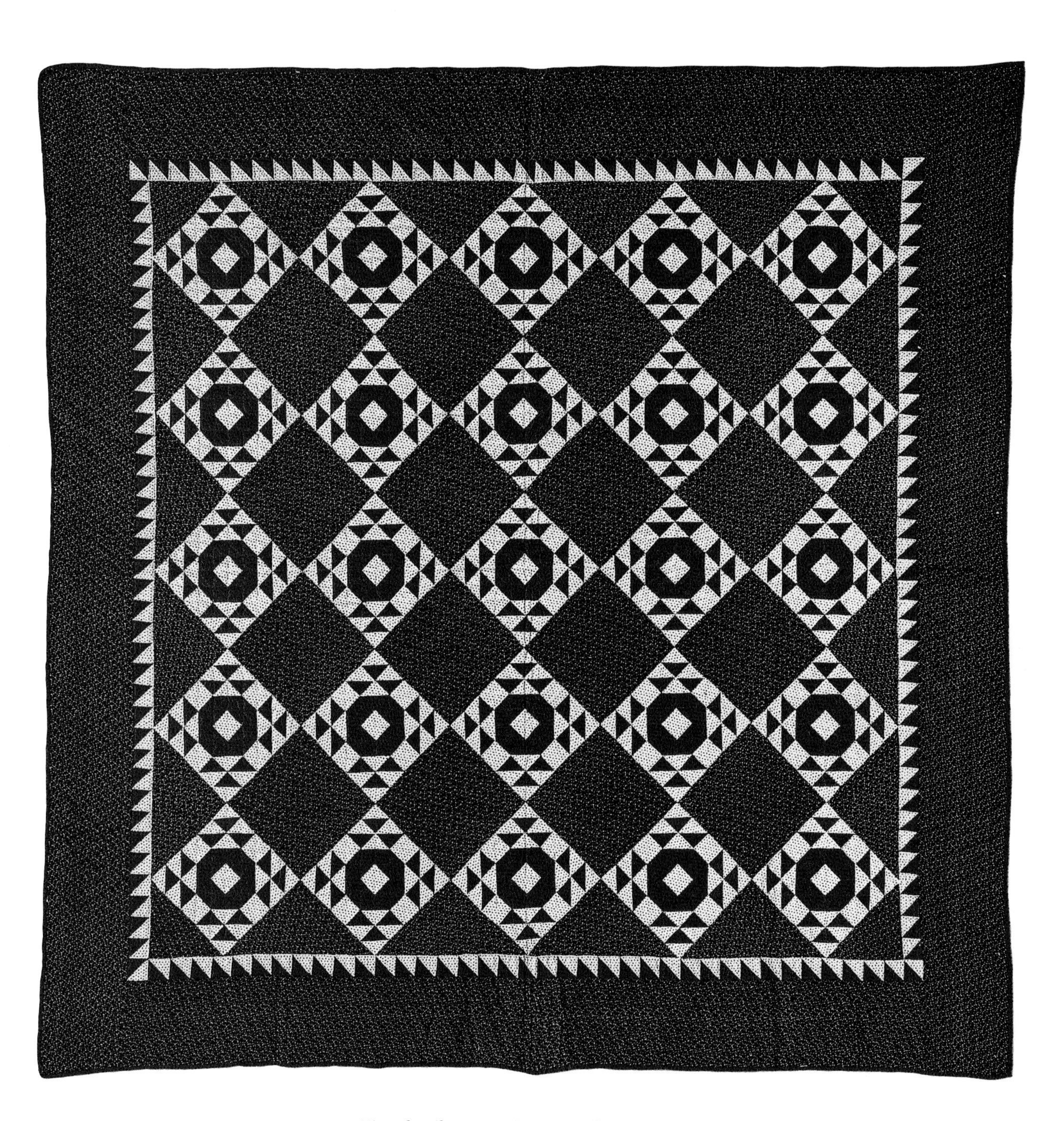

Pieced quilt, cotton, Lancaster County, c. 1920.

Bill Hentosh

HAPPY WITH HORSES. While the rest of the world whizzes past, most Amish families prefer the steady gait of a good horse for everyday transportation and help with the farming chores.

Clothesline Fills Up Fast With 12 Children at Home

◆ PROFILE ◆

Levi and Katie Hochstetler and their 12 children raise hogs on their 14-acre farm near LaGrange. Levi and two of the boys, Mervin and Harley, work at different factories. Daughter Barbara teaches school, and daughters Arlene and Malinda both work on a neighboring tomato farm. Daughter Dorothy helps at home and in the small variety store run by diarist Katie.

We got up at 4:15, our usual time, and got most of the children up.

I soon had Levi's breakfast of egg and cold cereal ready, and while he ate, the girls and I fixed his lunch and the boys went out to milk the cow and feed the pigs, horses and chickens.

Levi left for work with his driver at 5:10. We then fixed nine more lunches and got breakfast ready while the boys cleaned up. In the meantime, we got the younger ones up in time to eat breakfast with the rest of us, which was also eggs and cold cereal. Mervin then left for work at 5:50 and Harley left at 6.

Barbara wasn't at home this morning as she got back late last night from a trip to Wisconsin and spent the night at Forks Valley School, where she teaches. (There is a boarding room right in the schoolhouse.)

The schoolchildren washed the breakfast dishes and got ready for school. At 7:30, Alvin, 12, had the pony, "Browny", hitched to the two-wheel school buggy. Erma, 14, Wilma, 11, Lena, 9, and Sueanna, 7, joined him and they started for their 3-mile trip to school. Just as they were leaving, the station wagon drove in to pick up Arlene and Malinda.

Before breakfast I had started the fire in the kitchen cookstove which heats our piped water. After breakfast, Dorothy and I sorted the wash. The girls usually do the washing, but this morning I said I would do the washing if Dorothy did some baking.

When the girls heard this, they said, "Mother is going to do the washing. She probably doesn't even know how! How many years was it since she last washed?" Lena piped up, "It was probably 50 years ago!"

It was a perfect wash day—the clothes dried quickly, making room on the lines for more. Although we had washed last Friday, it seemed no end to the dresses—there were 30 dresses on the line.

Dorothy kept busy in the kitchen all day. She made a batch of granola, baked four loaves of plain white bread, four loaves of zucchini bread and made several pounds of butter.

Arlene did the ironing in the afternoon, but I thought it was too nice to sit in the house to do the mending, so I went out and cleaned out a flower bed and replanted some flower bulbs.

Mervin came home from work at 2:45, grabbed his bow and arrow and headed for the woods. Deer bow season opened last Friday.

Levi came home and worked on an oilstove and also on a gas iron. He has to fix them both for other people. Malinda came home at 2:40 and said they're done harvesting tomatoes for this year. She got the remainder of the wash in and folded or hung on hangers.

The schoolchildren came home at 3:30. Erma and Sueanna helped Malinda to get the wash away, and Wilma and Lena washed Dorothy's dirty dishes. After that was done, they set the table for supper.

Son Perry and his wife Susie came and had supper with us. They were anxious to hear about our trip to Wisconsin last Thursday to attend a wedding.

While we were enjoying a supper of mashed potatoes, gravy, candied carrots, chicken, zucchini bread, coleslaw, fresh peaches, zucchini brownies and pumpkin pie, we were busy talking, too.

After we were all done eating, we were still sitting at the table talking about our trip. Finally, I said, "Now if you men would help with the dishes, we could go on and talk about the trip while we're washing."

It was quickly decided that they were done talking about the trip, so, we women did the dishes, like usual.

As soon as Perry and Susie were out of the house, the children ran for their beds. It was 10:30 by the time Levi and I said good night.

Early Risers Enjoy Active Days

◆ PROFILE ◆

Clayton and Ann Knepp grow wheat, corn, alfalfa and sorghum, raise about 80 heifers and beef cattle and milk 35 cows on their farm near Haven. There are always 2-18 calves to bottle- or bucket-feed, but that's not the favorite chore of children Lorinda, 17, Andrew, 16, Eva, 13, and David, 11. "Those calves are so slobbery and impatient!" diarist Ann explains.

That shrill alarm is always such a rude awakening, and when it buzzes this morning at 4:30, I just want to turn over and go back to sleep. But I get up reluctantly and light the kerosene lamp on the dresser and then the two Coleman lanterns in the kitchen used for choring.

Last evening we had supper with friends and didn't get home very early, so I expect everyone to be draggin' this morning. I have time to clean Clayton's and my Sunday shoes and sit down to read *Our Daily Bread* devotional while the rest of the family slowly wake up and get out of bed.

Wearing a sweatshirt under my denim jacket, I step outside and gaze upward to check out the sky—clear, bright moonshine, stars a'twinkling. Looks like a beautiful day is in store. I hold my lantern up to read the thermometer—52°.

Usually the dogs, "Buster" and "Benji", greet us as we come out, but I see they're preoccupied with a dead cottontail this morning. Andrew and David soon join us. David puts feed at each cow's stanchion while I put milkers and strainers together.

Clayton is out getting the cows roused and herded into the holding pen. He has the propane light in the milking barn already lit.

Andrew heads out back to do the hog chores, then throw hay to the weaned calves and feed the rabbits.

David and I let in the four driving horses, "Cindy", "Lady", "Charlie" and "Faye"—also "Pat", the pony. About a month ago we purchased Cindy and Lady in Indiana, and our other horses haven't fully accepted them yet. This morning Charlie gets a little feisty, kicking out at Lady, so we call in Andrew for some assistance in getting them tied up.

Eva comes out to help her dad in the barn. He uses three units to milk the 30 Holsteins but needs a helper to feed them, wash and dip teats, take off hobbles and finally let cows out.

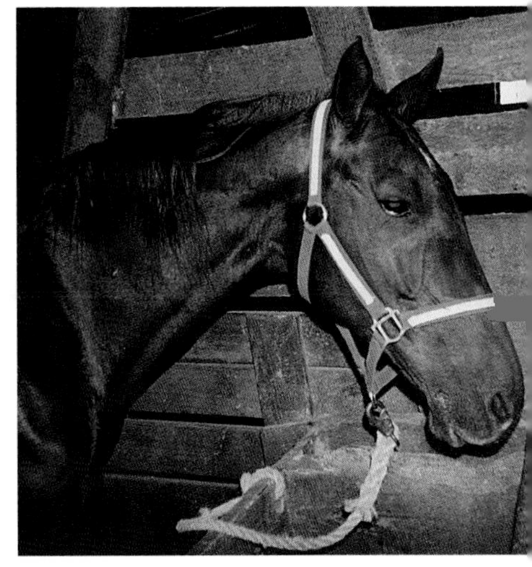

BOSS OF THE BARN. "Charlie", one of the Knepps' four driving horses, had a hard time accepting newcomers "Cindy" and "Lady".

Meanwhile David and I fix milk replacer for the frisky black and white calves in "Calf Village", as we call the cluster of calf huts outside. There are six to bucket-feed, four on bottles and two in a separate shed that drink out of a trough.

By 6:30 I'm back in the house, getting breakfast started and daughter Lorinda out of bed. She usually keeps late hours on weekends as young folks so often do, so forget about gettin' her out early on a Monday morning! She spent the weekend with girlfriends and was to the young folks' singin' last evening.

While Eva gets her hair put up, David sets the table for me and fixes his lunch. (They serve hot lunches at the

GOBBLE IT UP. Ann's kitchen counters and basement shelves are filled with home-canned fruits, vegetables and meats, including family-favorite turkey—great with biscuits!

Photos by Carol Deurksen

HISTORIC HOME. Knepps' farmhouse, built in 1929, has upstairs dance floor once popular for area social gatherings.

PLAIN PEGS near kitchen door (left) are handy for hanging jackets and hats worn by nearly all Amish men.

small public school they attend, but David's such a picky eater and never eats his money's worth, so he carries his lunch.)

We're running a little late this morning, so Eva and David go ahead and eat before the guys come in. I sit down and read *Keys for Kids*, a children's devotional to them. The bus comes at 7:20 a.m.

Later, as the rest of us eat turkey-baloney patties, hash browns and eggs, Dad Knepp drives in. He's wondering if it would suit for Clayton and Andrew to come help finish filling their silo after lunch. We visit awhile, and it's past 8 o'clock when we leave the table.

Clayton goes out to greenchop a load of silage for the cows. Lorinda gathers up all the dirty laundry, sorts it and puts some in soak. Then she does the dishes and also washes off the cans of turkey baloney still sitting on the countertop from when I canned it last week.

I head right out to do some yard work. I have ladies coming over tomorrow afternoon for a Tupperware party, and I want to tidy up a bit. Picked some big branches and raked up smaller ones, then mowed the front yard.

Andrew rakes up the unsightly mess the eight big turkey gobblers left around the backyard. We butchered those last Wednesday, and I don't miss their gobble-gobble!

I wave to friendly milkman Mike as he drives in the lane. Soon as I'm done mowing, I go the milkhouse to wash out the bulk tank so it's ready for the evening milk.

As I return to the house, I pass Clayton and Andrew hitching up "Lady" to the open buggy. She's one of the new ones and quite spirited yet, so they put kicking straps on her today.

"Mending time—son David, 10, is very hard on pants..."

Clayton ties her to the hitchin' post, then comes in to count the alms money collected yesterday at Communion services. Because Clayton is the deacon, he is in charge of the church account and will take this along to Yoder to deposit. He's going after parts to repair the silage wagon.

I brush the boys' felt black Sunday hats and put 'em back on the closet shelf. There's a pair of pants on the open sewing machine, so I quick sew on the loose suspender, something I seem to do almost every week. Our 10-year-old David is very rough on pants!

As I close up the machine, I put the wooden rooster spool holder back on top and think of my 91-year-old grandma back in Indiana. The rooster used to be hers. Through the double windows I see that Lorinda has the lines pretty well filled with clean laundry. It's a gorgeous, sunny day ...wash should dry nicely.

About 11 o'clock, sister-in-law Carol stops by. She's in the area on business, so I invite her for lunch and she accepts.

Carol and her husband Maynard are Mennonite and live over an hour's drive away. We seldom see them except for evening family birthday get-togethers, so this is a rare happening.

We prepare creamed turkey and biscuits. Because I had several cans that didn't seal last week, we're eating lots of turkey stuff since then. There's some turkey liver left, so I fry that, too, but Carol says "Yuck!" and declines my offer to sample it. Biscuits, gravy and applesauce are enough for her!

After lunch, the guys leave to go fill silo, and I take Carol upstairs to show her the storeroom. I had Clayton build 

LIGHT READING. A sunny window provides light for daytime reading (above). At night, gas lamps (left) give rooms a warm glow.

me some shelves so I could organize better. So far, it's quite a mess yet—boxes are piled in the hall and in Eva's room, needing to be sorted through and some discarded.

Carol's never seen much of our upstairs, so I have to show her what's beyond the small corner door of the storeroom. She is awestruck as we step into a very large, unfinished room above our washhouse. It's filled with lots of dusty "junk"; things you think you might use someday. But Carol is too intrigued to notice the mess and even more so as I tell her the stories I've heard about this big room.

Elderly Amish from the community have told me how this used to be a gathering place for square dancing. There's a raised platform on the end where the guitar or banjo players and the "callers" would stand.

This house was built in 1929, according to a date on the foundation, and must hold many memories. We've had vanloads of Amish folks from other states drive in just to look around, telling us they knew the Planks, who used to live here.

After Carol goes on about her business, I realize I didn't bring in the mail yet, and I seldom forget that. I'm always anticipating news from "home", which is northern Indiana where I grew up and the rest of my family still lives.

Sure enough, there's a big fat letter from a special sister-in-law. So that calls for sit-down time, to have a silent chat on six pages of tablet paper.

The rest of the afternoon I do odds and ends, first baking two pumpkin roll cakes and fixing cream cheese filling, both to be served as refreshments tomorrow.

I wash out the four pails we used yesterday at Communion for the feet-washing ritual, dry them and carry them and the four white towels Lori washed today back up to the storeroom. Lori has most of the wash in and put away already.

The scholars come home about 3:30 and, as usual, are hungry. The girls raid David's lunch and finish up his leftovers while he fixes a bowl of graham crackers and milk. I hurry them up a bit. We have special plans for tonight and need to get to chores early.

Andrew comes home at 4:15. By then David has the barn ready and cows in so Andrew can start milking. The girls go out to do other chores, so I fold the pile of socks and get ready for the evening.

We were all too busy to celebrate Mom Knepp's birthday in September, so we're finally doing that tonight. The folks serve meals by reservation in their home, so going out to eat is a treat for them. Tonight, we're taking them to Furr's in Hutchinson.

Brother Gerald, also Mennonite, drives in about 6:30 p.m. with a load of youngsters—eight of 'em—for Lorinda and Andrew to baby-sit. Gerald picks up the folks, and the rest of us meet them in town—we've hired a van to take us.

"Today's mail brings a fat letter from a special sister-in-law..."

After eating heartily from the splendid buffet line, we all go to Wal-Mart yet and do some shopping. Back home, we find the house toy-strewn and Lorinda ready to turn the children all back to their parents!

We chat a bit about the evening, kneel for evening prayer and all head to bed. Past 10 o'clock already, so the alarm will be an unwelcome sound again come morning!

AFTER LUNCH I went with Floyd Beechy to move and set up the silage cutter. Then the excitement started.

I was riding with Floyd, pulling his power unit and ensilage cutter behind his sorrel Belgian team. We stopped at a filling station to fill our gas cans up, and I thought I'd treat Floyd and his son, Abe, who was following with the buggy, to ice cream. (I guess I've never met an Amishman yet who doesn't like ice cream.)

Then I rode on the buggy with Abe. As we started down the long hill out of Chesterhill, the shaft came loose from the buggy on the left side, which started the buggy swinging from side to side.

Abe pushed on the brake, which slid the buggy. We finally came to a stop on the wrong side of the road, headed toward a steep ditch. Thank the good Lord for a good, quiet horse!

When I got out of the buggy, my knees were weak and I was shaking so bad I could hardly put the bolt back into the axle clip. I rode the rest of the way to Joel's with Floyd.

—Warren Fussner, Stockport, Ohio

25,000 Fuzzy Balls Arrive On 'Chick Day' in Ohio

◆ PROFILE ◆

Wayne and Lydiann Miller live on the farm where Wayne grew up, 5 miles east of Millersburg. In 1989, the Millers began renting out their cropland and built a 40- x 500-foot poultry house in which they raise contract broilers. The Millers have three children: Nathan, 16, Matthew, 2, and Carolyn, 7 weeks. Diarist Wayne has been an ordained minister since 1978.

David Miller

OUT TO PASTURE. "Nip", one of the Millers' three driving horses, will soon retire at age 22.

Guta myah (Good Morning)—and it certainly is! Dawn is spreading out across a cloudless, cream-bordered blue sky as I make my way to the broiler house.

The early harvest moon is making its exit high in the western horizon. A sharp, frosty wind breezing across the lawn pats my cheek. Ah, this fresh country air! The temperature at 6:45 a.m. is 42°.

Son Nathan has already left for the siding company where he works. They do siding work all over the state, specializing in vinyl siding.

We're getting "visitors" today, and I want to make sure they'll have toasty warm facilities when they come. You guessed it—it's chick day! Scheduled arrival time is 9 a.m.

Our dog, "Buddy", gets his neck scratched as I pass by him on the way to the barn. An injury prevents him from getting to that itchy spot. The blue-heeler collie mix enjoys the attention.

Going by the house, I notice the brilliant colors of the marigolds in red-orange and yellow. The Dusty Millers strike a pretty pose among the geraniums of pink and red. The impatiens are trying to revive their strength after a duster from the first frost the other morning. The dazzling array of flowers in the early morning sun does lift one's soul.

The hog we're fattening greets me with a few grunts as I enter the barn. After feeding her with some leftover feed from the feed pans in the broiler house, I feed our three standardbreds.

"Nip", our faithful driver, is 22 years old. I've had him since I was 22. Then there's "Diamond", our 4-year-old. He's becoming the main one now as we ease the load off old Nip.

"Chip", another 4-year-old, greets me with a bang against the stall door. He'll probably go back to the horse dealer—he can't quite take these Holmes County hills.

Later, the natural gas engine is started to provide hydraulic power so Lydiann can begin her wash day. She finishes sorting as I carry down the diaper pail per her request.

Our little girlie Carolyn is awake now, so Lydiann feeds her while I eat a quick breakfast of cold cereal. Later we have our devotional period together, a reading of a chapter in the Bible, and prayer. We believe strongly that "prayer is the key to the day and the lock for the night."

Next, Matthew is up. I get him dressed after rocking Carolyn to sleep for Lydiann so she can continue washing. I take Matthew along out to the broiler house to await the chicks' arrival from the Strasburg, Ohio, hatchery.

Here come the chicks! After spending about 50 minutes to unload, the two delivery men wave good-bye. How many do we have? 25,000 little fuzzy balls. I finish letting down the paper barriers and water lines, etc. Now we're settled for another 7 weeks.

After a lunch of leftover noodles with mixed-in chicken and peas, cooked graham (stone-ground wheat) and homemade yogurt, I go to the barn and let the horses out into the north pasture.

The afternoon is spent cleaning out their pens and also the hog pen. I put the manure down into the shed where the heifers had been. They were sold last week. Later, I'll clean out the whole shed, using the neighbor's horses and my spreader.

Lydiann gathers in the drying wash to put it all away. Her niece, Miriam Yoder, stops by to visit on her way home from a neighboring family where church services were held on Sunday.

Returning home from work, Nathan goes on an exploration trek to a neighboring woods to see if he can see any squirrel activity. Back home later, he cleans out a small flower bed for Lydiann.

I chase the standardbreds back into the barn, and Nathan puts them into their respective stalls. The sliding door buggy is put in its place again. I've checked on the chicks throughout the day, and they're doing well so far.

After a supper of chicken and biscuits with pear salad, we spend the evening in relaxation before "hitting the sack".

Gute Nacht! (Good Night!) 

Muscle and Memories Mix at...
An Amish Auction

THERE'S excitement in the air...along with the delicious aromas of homemade doughnuts, pies, baked beans, potato salad and barbecue.

A nearby field is filled with farm machines—most of them horse-drawn. Some folks reminisce about using them...others look for bargains because they still do.

But the biggest attraction is the horses. *Big* horses. As they are paraded past, in pairs or singly, "oohs" and "aahs" are heard from the farm folks standing shoulder to shoulder.

Some come to buy, others just to look and talk and eat and enjoy. And everyone leaves satisfied. Says one smiling farmer: "I'll take an Amish auction anytime—it's better than state fair!"

—Julie Habel, Holy Cross, Iowa

Forced to Slow Down, He's a Patient Observer

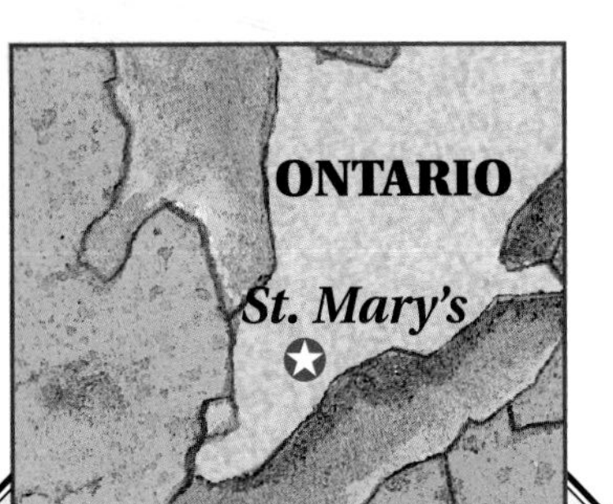

◆ PROFILE ◆

Yost and Katie Yoder milk 15 cows and grow oats, barley, corn and hay on their 100-acre farm near St. Mary's. In addition, Yost and his brother, Enos, run a carpentry business along with two of their neighbors. The Yoders have five children: Nathan, 15, Alvin, 14, Ephriam, 11, Rosanna, 5, and Ella Mae, 2. Yost kept this diary.

So here hath been dawning another new day. Think, wilt thou let it slip useless away?

At 6 a.m. the eastern sky is showing signs of a sunny day. Looking out my window, I see lights in the barn, and I hear the diesel running, so the milking must be underway.

Sleeping in like this might sound great, but after 4 weeks of it, I am looking forward very much to making that trip out to the barn every morning. According to the doctor, it might go another 2 months before that happens, though.

You see, on September 2, I fell from a house roof we were shingling and broke my femur, the bone between my knee and hip. Instead of a cast on my leg, the surgeon installed a steel rod in my bone so I can get around some on crutches. So today's activities will be mostly given as observed from my bed in the living room.

The sounds and smells coming from the kitchen indicate Katie is in from the barn. Oh, but the wood fire in the kitchen stove feels good as I hobble out to the kitchen.

At 7 a.m. the temperature shows 55° with a brisk westerly wind blowing. My sister Amanda has now gone out the lane to her job for the day. She drives their horse, "Rusty", the 5 miles to where she works part-time at a chicken processing plant where they custom dress chickens.

After a hearty breakfast, I think I'll go back to my headquarters, my hospital bed. These days it serves as office, library, sleeping quarters and rest area.

Jim Bickell now drives in, and, after loading ladders and tools, my brother Enos and Ivan Hochstetler leave with Jim for work. They'll likely finish putting on a house roof 2 miles from here. Neighbor Joe Coblentz is also a member of our carpenter crew, but today he will take my place at filling silo instead.

Teachers Mary Yoder and Laura Coblentz give a friendly wave as they leave their horse in our barn and then pass our house on their way to school. Built in 1970, our one-room school has 28 pupils in grades one through eight this term.

Next I see Nathan heading out with the team and wagon to fill silo at Coblentz's. Four of us neighbors help together to fill six silos, and this is the last farm with two more silos to fill. Corn is an excellent crop this year, which makes for fast silo filling

Seeing Nathan, my mind goes back to June 16, 1978 when both he and "Belle", our black Percheron mare, were born. I sure was a happy father and farmer when both my first son and first foal arrived that day! They have since both caused some trying moments, but thinking back, they have both been a great pleasure to work (and play) with.

> STORY TIME is precious to both Gramma and the grandchildren.
>
> Today's story was about a little girl who had a bad habit of grumbling and not appreciating what she had. Her mother took her out to a park and tried to reason with her.
>
> A balloon man came by, and the mother told her daughter she would buy a balloon for every blessing she could think of. Soon, the man had sold all his balloons and the blessings were still not all told! A good lesson for us all, starting with me!
>
> *—Mary Schlabach*
> *Millersburg, Ohio*

Now Alvin, grade eight, and Ephraim, grade six, are joined by Vernon, grade eight, Karen, grade seven, and Elmer, grade three, as they race out the lane toward school.

With Katie washing the laundry, Rosanna and Ella Mae outside playing and most everyone else at work or school, our morning rush is over. Now I will try to get some mail ready.

Lunchtime already! I think all I need is a glass of milk and a sandwich. My sister Elizabeth Hochstetler comes to spend the afternoon with my mother or perhaps my sister-in-law Rosemary, who had an operation last week on her ankle and also isn't very mobile at this time. My niece, Amanda Yoder, is helping her out with her housework.

Now comes one of the highlights of my day—it's mail time. Let's see, there's a letter from my brother Noah, who lives in Virginia...one from my nephew Alvin Yoder from Delaware... and two *Budgets*, one dated September 15 and one September 22. Guess they'll have to be read someday when I'm not so busy.

With brothers or sisters living in Delaware, Michigan, Oklahoma, Pennsylvania, Virginia and Wisconsin, plus many relatives and friends in other parts of the U.S., the *Budget* is an interesting paper in our family.

Later our neighbors, Ken and Ann McLellan, stop in for a visit. I do get a lot of visitors and sure appreciate them all. And now the children are home from school already.

The boys do their chores, which include gathering eggs, washing the milk tank, getting silage and feed ready for the cows, getting hay down for the colts in the barn, feeding their rabbits, etc. Seems there's always work on a farm, but also some time for play.

I see Alvin is now out with his pel-

app

BROKEN LEG has prevented diarist Yost from helping the neighbors fill their silos and assisting wife Katie with garden harvest, but it's given him time to read, write and reflect.

David Troyer

Amos Graber

let rifle hunting down some pesky starlings. Grandmother gives the boys five cents per starling, and with their dad supplying the pellets, each bird is clear profit...quite different than farming!

Poor Ephraim—he still has to fill the wood box. Seems there's no younger brother around to take over that tedious job. Well, perhaps in a few years Dad will have to.

Amanda is now home from her long day at work. Soon it is time for supper—buttercup squash and sweet potatoes from our garden, noodles, steak and applesauce.

Afterward I stand on one leg and wash most of the dishes while Rosanna dries them. Katie and the two boys go to the barn to help with the milking.

With the day's work done, the family gathers in the living room to discuss the day's activities. Enos brings measurements over for another job, so I hope to get a list of materials and a price ready for him tomorrow. We also discuss some future jobs and work in general.

Enos and I have played and worked together all our lives. I was 3 years old and Enos was 1 when we moved here with our parents in 1959 from Dover, Delaware.

With our visitors gone and the children all in bed, Katie helps me with my exercises. I am working on my leg muscles trying to get them to function properly again.

Now lying here in bed with the house all quiet, there's an almost full moon shining in my window. Looking out, the scenery is simply gorgeous. There is a neighborhood dog barking occasionally in the distance, and I hear the soft hoot of an owl from one of the maple trees in the lawn.

God has surely been good to us—do I appreciate all His goodness enough? My eyes are getting heavy, so I now wish all people everywhere much health and happiness. *Gute Nacht.*

Out of eternity this new day was born, into eternity, at night, to return!

Chores Follow 'Morning Rush Hour'

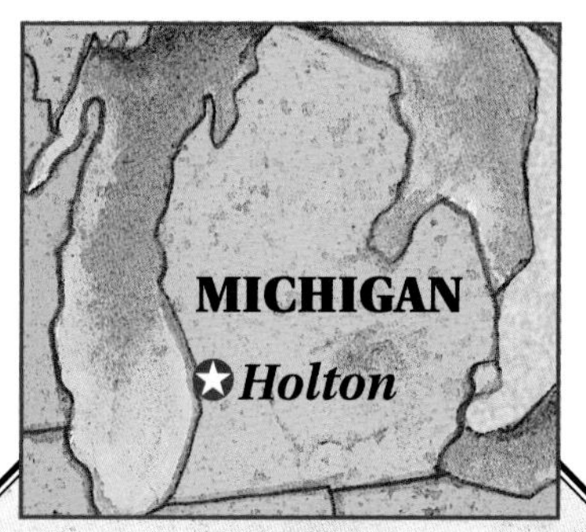

◆ **PROFILE** ◆

Joseph and Lizzie Kauffman feed 1,000 hogs a year and raise and dress out homegrown fryers on their 30-acre farm near Holton. The men in the family also repair pallets several days a week. The Kauffmans' children are Amzie Ray, 16, Milo Ray, 15, Sylvia Sue, 14, Lizzie Ellen, 12, and Katie Ann, 11. Lizzie kept this diary.

The alarm jangled at 5:30, awakening the family to a crisp, cool morning and putting into motion the daily hubbub of getting Sylvia, Ellen and Katie Ann off to school by 8:15.

As Ellen hurried to the outdoor john, she took a moment to stare into space, appreciating the bright morning moon, and came bounding in the door with, "Mom, I found the Little Dipper!"

Amzie and Milo slowly emerged from hibernation and fed the horses and pumped pig water while Daddy made a breakfast of toast, eggs, peaches and cookies.

He loves to cook. One of his specialties is pancakes, which we have frequently. Tomato gravy and biscuits often find their way to the table, too.

This morning's meal had been planned for oatmeal, but when the girls opened the milk jug with upturned noses and some awful noises, we vetoed anything made with milk!

The girls got dressed for school. Then Sylvia and Ellen packed seven lunches with egg sandwiches, yellow sweet cherries, cookies and brownies. Katie Ann set the table and I did—well, I'm not quite sure just what I did, except this and that, as mothers do!

Breakfast was eaten at 7, followed by family devotions, after which "Fern", the black standardbred, was hooked to the buggy and the boys headed for Mast's mini barns, where we have a pallet repair business.

Before heading out for school, the girls attended to their usual morning duties of dishes, sweeping and a general reddin' up of the house.

"Kate", our faithful 10-year-old Haflinger-Welsh pony cross was then hooked to the school buggy, and *pitter-pat-pitter-pat* off to the school they went.

Sighing with relief that another 

morning "rush hour" was past, I donned my old coat, scarf and boots and headed for the hog lot to help Joe sort hogs for market.

Next we headed for the horse barn to harness "Rodapple Mark", our Percheron stallion, and "Gypsy Rose", a Percheron mare. These two were then hooked to the wagon to deliver some hay to the remaining horses out in the pasture.

Afterward, we went out our long driveway, which has a cornfield on one side and pasture and woods on the other, to go over to Mast's and help the boys do pallets. Just as we turned onto the road, the feed truck arrived, so we did a U-turn and came back in to help unload.

While waiting on the man and watching the horses, I decided I needed another coat and some gloves.

We finally headed for the pallet shop, about 4 miles away, and arrived there around 11. The boys already had a good start, but we still put in a long day's work to get all the rest of that load finished.

A treat of potato salad and bananas was added to our lunch this afternoon, thanks to a neighbor lady from a local church who brought out some leftover food to Alvin Mast's, consisting of salad, bananas, lettuce and a bunch of unmarked No.10 cans of food.

We worked on pallets till 5:30, then loaded some scrap wood onto the wagon to use for firewood in the stove and also to heat my laundry water in an outdoor iron kettle.

The boys headed home with Fern and the buggy, and Joe and I brought the wagon, stopping at four different homes on the way to share the leftover food with others.

When the girls came home from school at 3:30, Ellen and Katie Ann fed the 300 1-month-old fryers and attended to the laying hens. While those two were choring, Sylvia stirred up four batches of homemade grapenuts cereal, which is baked as a cake (eight pans full) then cooled, run through a salad master and toasted in the oven to provide many more delicious breakfasts to come.

"Feed truck arrived just as we were leaving, so we did a U-turn..."

Having finished their assigned tasks, the girls headed to the neighbor's to bring home some of our canned meat that is stored in their basement. (We live in a trailer and have no basement of our own.)

Our supper was toasted cheese sandwiches and tomato juice, which we had after 8 when the boys came in from deer hunting in the woods.

By 9, we called it a day and headed for the blessings of another night's rest with plenty of warm covers, awaiting another jingle from the alarm at 5:30 tomorrow.

Don Shenk

❖ Why Buggies, Not Cars? ❖

ONE of the things first noticed in any Amish area is the black buggies, and one of the questions most often asked is why these "plain people" persist at using this outdated form of transportation.

We asked about this in several Amish communities and got these answers:

First of all, not all Amish buggies are black. In fact, there are more than 90 different kinds of buggies in the Amish communities around the U.S. There are orange buggies, brown buggies, closed one-seaters and two-seaters, open one-seaters and two-seaters and racy two-wheelers that look a bit like racing sulkies.

Still, they're all buggies, and the Amish hold fast to these antiquated vehicles for some specific reasons.

First, they recognize that the buggy is slow compared to the automobile. That fits in well with their slower-paced, calmer approach to life in general, and has an additional benefit:

The horse can pull a buggy about 10 miles an hour, and after 20 miles or so it must be given a good rest lasting several hours. Due to this limitation in time and distance, a buggy driver is pretty much restricted to his community—he cannot easily reach distant cities where "modern" life-styles might tempt him.

Echoing that philosophy was a conversation overheard between a tourist and an elderly Amish man in Lancaster, Pennsylvania: "With that horse and buggy, there's no way you can get to Pittsburgh or Philadelphia," said the tourist. "We know," said the Amish man, "we know."

The Amish also recognize that different types of cars have become a status symbol among their "English" (non-Amish) neighbors. Amish buggies have such minor differences that they avoid this class distinction.

And after explaining these reasons, the Amish often smile and add, "The horse reproduces itself, while the car produces nothing but debt and expense."

Kitchen Chores Fill the Morning

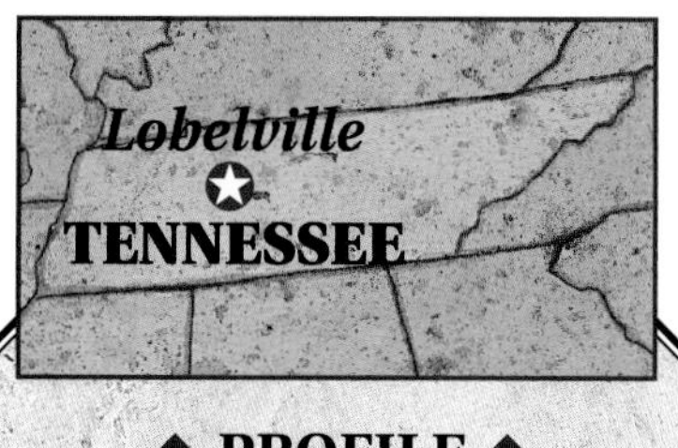

◆ PROFILE ◆

Diarist Elizabeth Byler lives with sister Susie Glick and her husband Levi on their small farm in Lobelville. The Glicks grow hay and raise cattle, sheep and goats; Levi is also a farrier and shoes horses twice a week.

Sherry Pardee

BUSY BAKER. Bread baking day got off to a sorry start when flour was spilled on the floor, but "help" kneading dough from little niece and nephew made diarist Elizabeth smile anyway.

At 6 a.m. Levi left to help a neighbor build a fence. Wagons were already rumbling past on their way to one or the other of the three sorghum mills nearby to start pressing cane.

After breakfast I went to get the bucket of whole wheat flour out of the pantry to make bread...and promptly dropped it! Flour swooshed across the floor. After cleaning up the mess, I had to go next door to borrow a few cups of flour, as I'd dumped just as much as I needed!

Susie's children, Lydianne, 4, and Harvey, 2, got up before I was done making the bread, so after Susie had them dressed, they had to sit upon the counter next to me to watch like they always do.

When I had enough flour in the dough, I beat it with a rolling pin. All at once Harvey so innocently asked, "What did the bread do?" He thought I was paddling it! I had to laugh and give him a big hug.

Susie made her bed and the children's cribs that are in her room, then gave the children their breakfast. They wanted pancakes.

Instead of doing the laundry, we decided to cut up a bushel of small yellow Delicious apples from Dad Byler's orchard and make applesauce.

Meantime, the children were outside, chasing a hen with chicks till we stopped them. Next they played on the new swing Susie put up for them in front of the house. But when they discovered us making applesauce, they had to "help".

We let them put the quartered apples into the large stainless steel stock pot. When they tired of that, they got bowls and pans out of the big oak cupboard, lined them up on the couch and "cooked and cooked".

Finally, they got water out of the bathroom to wash the dishes. We put a stop to that as we didn't want a wet couch!

For dinner we had fresh bread right out of the oven. Oh, the wonderful smell and taste of fresh wheat bread can't be beat!

> ***"Lydianne, 4, and Harvey, 2, had to watch like they always do..."***

Right after dinner, we cleared the table, and I set up the Victoria strainer to puree the apples that had cooked while we ate. The children continued to "help"—Harvey got up on a chair and cranked the handle while Lydianne kept the chute clear with a rubber spatula. Every now and then, she'd bang it onto the pan, sending applesauce flying.

Later, while Susie put the sauce in jars and closed them up, the children hauled wood to the big black iron kettle out behind the house, where we processed the 19 quarts of sauce for 20 minutes.

This afternoon I had planned to visit the sorghum mill...but on my way to the pasture to get "Pat", the buggy horse, I stepped in a fresh cow pie with my good shoes!

After I'd gotten cleaned up, I noticed Pat didn't have a halter on. I tried to get him to go up to the barn, but he kept swinging away from me until all at once, WHAM! His big hooves came flying for my face!

I quickly shielded myself with my arms, which took a painful blow. Still, I felt fortunate—it could have been serious had I been standing only a few inches closer.

Finally, with Susie's help, I caught, harnessed and hitched Pat to our open buggy. I took off for the mill and she and the children got to lie down for their naps.

At the Beachy sorghum mill, the stripping gang of about 15 people was taking a break around the water jug. The cane looked so nice, standing straight and tall with all the leaves pulled off.

Up the hill behind the cooking shed, 

the boys were just done pressing for the day. The horses had been unhitched from the two 2-horse presses, and the cane pummies (pressed out stalks) were being laid aside. They will be used to mulch raspberry patches or else dried and used for bedding.

In the main cooking shed, Simon Beachy was firing the huge furnace with pieces of wood 4 feet long. His sons Dennis and Paul were letting out the molasses into containers. It sure boiled up nicely and came off so thick you could almost chew it. (Southerners want their sorghum so thick they can "wrap it around a post", as the saying goes.)

I brought home a load of sorghum cane heads, and we unloaded them into the hay mow with the hay track. Levi will feed the cane heads to his seven head of cows this winter. They sure look forward to those.

Next Levi did his chores of feeding goats, sheep and the dog. Then we ate supper. Susie made vegetable soup casserole, which is a meal in itself. She adds gravy to her home-canned soup, puts scratch biscuits on top and bakes it. We also had applesauce, radishes, lettuce and vanilla pudding with bananas and graham crackers mixed in.

After dinner, we sat down to visit a little while, and I scanned through the *Budget*.

Lydianne hung onto my dress tail all evening to make sure I'd keep my promise that she could sleep with me tonight. While she waited on me to finish this diary before going to bed, she got out some dishes and nearly filled my bed with them and played "cooking"! My, it takes a lot of patience with these energetic little ones.

I helped her clear them away so we could get to bed soon after 10.

Betty Smithhart

OUR DAY was filled with visitors.

Brother Reuben's wife, Emma, and three little girls came over before lunch to get a pattern to make rocking chair covers. Mom treated them each with an apple before they went home.

Later, two Englishmen came and brought us a deer which they had skinned and asked if they could hunt here in exchange. Rudy got the wash in, then Mattie folded it and did the ironing.

We had a surprise this afternoon when Alvin Lambright Jr. of Berne drove in and will be spending here till Wednesday. He will be going with our brothers and us girls to the Lexington horse sale tomorrow.

Since bow season opened Saturday, he also brought his bow along and went hunting this afternoon with Amos after he came home from school. Amos hunts with a crossbow. They didn't have any luck. Meanwhile, Simon cleaned the lunch pails and went out and played with the pony colt he's training to neck rein.

Later this afternoon, Mrs. Cletus Christner and three of her children came to get the copper kettle to cook apple butter. The kettle belongs to Jake W. Schwartz, but we had borrowed it to cook our apple butter. We treated them with cookies while we visited.

Mary and I stopped quilting in time to do the patching and help with supper. We had hamburger patties, fried potatoes, gravy, homemade cottage cheese, plus greens from the garden, which were tomatoes, lettuce, radishes and sweet peppers. Our dessert was cookies and blueberry cheese cake.

After Dad and the boys came home from work, they went back in the field and set corn in shocks, while Rudy and Simon did the chores. We enjoyed our evening by visiting and eating watermelons that we raised. Mary and I each took turns using the trampoline before going to bed.

—Lizzie Wickey, Bennington, Indiana

CHAPTER THREE

Pieced quilt, cotton, made by Amelia G. Hesler
of Penn Township, Lancaster County, c. 1900-1920.

Bill Hentosh

HOME FROM SCHOOL. Although Amish children in some communities ride on public busses, most, like the boys above, get to and from school the old-fashioned way—by walking.

Neighbors Rely on In-Home Food Market

◆ PROFILE ◆

Lovina Miller, who is unmarried, keeps house for her widowed father Dennis, 78. Their small farm is being worked by a nephew who grows oats, corn and hay and raises dairy heifers. Dennis, retired from farming, maintains a shop where he repairs small engines. Lovina runs a bulk grocery store in their home and also does quilting.

Eli Miller

TIME TO STOCK UP. In her small market similar to the one above, diarist Lovina Miller repackages bulk foods into smaller containers. Customers pause for some friendly conversation.

Woke at the usual time, 5 a.m., and got the heating stove and kitchen range fires started. Nights are getting chilly, and wood heat feels pretty good.

It was a beautiful morning. We had frost last week, so the trees are getting their pretty fall colors.

Dad got up about 6, and we had breakfast of oatmeal with a cookie and tea. Then I did the dishes and straightened up the house while Dad went out to his shop, where he repairs small motors.

Today I needed to do a lot of bagging up in my bulk food store. (I buy in large amounts and bag it in smaller quantities.) My first customer arrived at 7:30 to buy flour, yeast, oatmeal and a 60-pound pail of corn syrup. She will have church next Sunday and needs to do a lot of baking.

I had another eight customers this forenoon. At 11:30 I fixed our dinner of boiled potatoes, green beans, meatballs with gravy, tapioca pudding and peaches. But we didn't get to eat till after 1, as we both had customers during the noon hour. Some days I wonder when other people eat!

In the afternoon, my sister and her daughter came for supplies, so we needed to chat awhile, too. She will be feeding a silo-filling crew on Tuesday.

Later, an "English" lady came by with some material for her quilt. Quilts are my sideline.

After her, UPS came with supplies to be priced and put away. By then, it was time to tend to fires and take a break till several more customers came.

At 5:30, I made supper of fish soup and fish sandwiches, leftover pudding and peaches. After dishes, I did more weighing out of Jell-O and powdered sugar till 8 o'clock, then wrote my *Budget* letter and did some reading till 9 o'clock bedtime.

BY THE TIME I got dressed and straightened up the kitchen, it was time for Kenton Dale Lemon to come. He's the 2-year-old that husband Obed and I baby-sit each day from 7:30 a.m. to 4:30 p.m. while his parents work.

It seems no two days are alike as we do our chores according to Kenton's needs. He's a very nice and obedient boy and a pleasure to have around...but he is all boy. We raised six boys of our own, and Kenton brings back many memories. It only takes him half a day to give the house a lived-in look!

Before I got started with laundry this morning, Kenton decided he wanted popcorn. Whenever Kenton starts begging for popcorn, it pleases Obed. I popped some for them, and after their snack, Kenton sat on Obed's lap and fell asleep.

When Kenton woke up, I fixed lunch for us. Afterward we went outdoors to bring in the clothes that needed to be ironed. Kenton was wearing the new red cowboy boots his parents just bought for him, and he watched his boots so much, he walked right into an evergreen bush!

Lots of times Kenton wears Obed's hat when he rides our plastic horse on wheels. He and our granddaughter Linda, 5, get along very well, even though he speaks English and she speaks partly Pennsylvania Dutch. Anymore he doesn't even have to ask me what she's saying.

—Verna Troyer, Holmesville, Ohio

Several Sidelines Keep This Large Family Busy

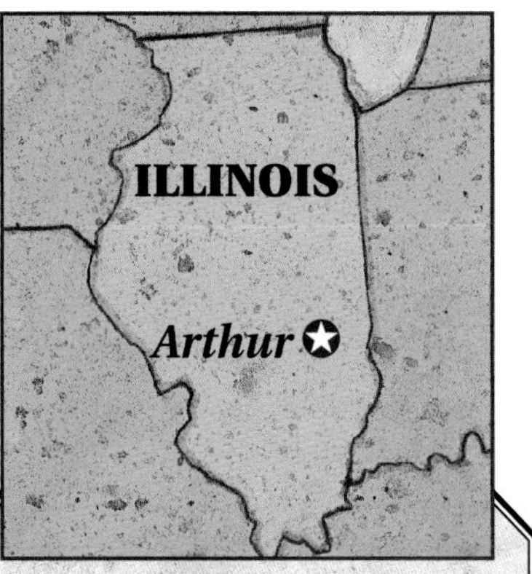

◆ PROFILE ◆

Andy and Vera Jess live on a 5-acre farm in Douglas County. Andy works at CHI Overhead Doors in nearby Arthur, and Vera cooks and serves meals to tourists and guests in the settlement. As a family hobby, the Jesses make and hand-paint animal pull toys to sell. Andy and Vera have 6 children: Lizzie Ann, 20, Paul, 17, Ruby Fern, 16, Ernest, 14, Mary Louise, 13, and Myron, 11. Vera kept this diary.

The alarm went off at 4 a.m., and my day began by going out and getting the morning paper, skimming through the pages, checking births and deaths.

By 4:30, I started fixing the lunches, lining them up by the door in order as the family leaves. At 5:30, I made a round through the house waking everyone up, and soon afterward we sat down to our breakfast of fried potatoes, tomato gravy and cold cereal.

"Last night we had 60 friends here for supper..."

By 6 o'clock, after family devotions, Lizzie's ride came to take her to work at Riverside Door Shop. Five minutes later, Paul's ride came to head to Okaw Truss Factory. Shortly thereafter, Andy and Ernest left on their bikes. (They only have 3 miles or so to work).

Ruby and Mary cleared away the dishes while Myron went out to do the morning chores with the horses, chickens and dogs. We raise cocker spaniels and shelties and presently have six shelties that are 7 weeks old.

I took my morning walk of 2 miles; time to myself to clear my thoughts on such a beautiful day. When I got back, the school bus came and picked up Mary, eighth grade, and Myron, sixth grade.

I had a lot of leftover food to take care of this morning as we had church here yesterday in our basement. Had four 14-foot tables set up after services, and all filled twice, plus a few more. Our light lunch consisted of homemade white and wheat bread, also boughten bread, butter, peanut butter spread, strawberry jam, cheese spread, egg salad, pickled red beets, fresh tomatoes, chunked apple schnitz and coffee.

TIDY TRANSPORTATION. Jess family members keep buggies clean and ready to use in large garage near the farmhouse (top). Sideline business raising dogs keeps kennel (center) filled.

After that, I dug the sweet potatoes and canned the red beets and tomatoes that were left over from yesterday while Ruby got the wash in and folded.

At 4 when the schoolchildren and Lizzie came home, we four women all biked over to F&B Woodworking to clean their offices, lunchroom and rest rooms, a weekly job for us.

Myron gathered up the sweet potatoes and washed them, plus did his evening chores. After work Andy and Paul took the hay wagons out of the horse yard (where the horses were tied up yesterday) and took them home to the neighbors.

MORNING RITUAL. After setting the table for breakfast (above), diarist Vera Jess prepares lunches and lines them up near the back door in the order in which they'll be picked up (right).

After dishes were washed, I passed around cookies to all those who helped with the dishes and to those who *didn't* (the men!).

In the evening we had invited friends, and the youngsters also invited their friends. Had around 60 here for scalloped potatoes with ham, dressing, ham and cheese sandwiches, vegetable pizza, Jell-O apple salad, cream cheese pudding, cherry and raspberry pie and ice cream. After supper, the young folks left for the singing at another place that also had church.

While I cleaned up today, Ruby was doing the laundry and getting it out on the line to dry. When she was done, we had a light lunch and a rest.

Ernest went to Omer Kuhn's after work to help with their chores, being as they are so busy with the harvest. He didn't come home again till almost dark.

It was 7:30 before we finally got to eat our supper of potatoes, dressing and pie.

Dishes were soon washed and showers taken. By 9, everyone retired to bed, tired from our busy day.

500 Guests to be Welcomed at Wedding

◆ **PROFILE** ◆

William and Nina Bontrager grow corn and hay and raise hogs and sell feeder pigs on their 28-acre farm near Hicksville, Ohio. In addition, William works at M & W Countertop Shop. The Bontragers have five children: Mary Louise, 21, Lavern, 20, Leonard, 19, Leona, 17, and Samuel, 15. Nina kept this diary.

Tthe clock struck 5 a.m. and I awoke with a start. We can't over-sleep this morning—only 4 more days till the wedding day of our oldest daughter, Mary Louise.

Before sunrise, I was in the garden digging the last of the potatoes and watching the sun come up. It was such a lovely sight and a good time to meditate.

William will not go to work this week, as there is far too much work to be done around home with only one thing on our minds: the wedding!

He came to the garden and advised me to let Albert (Mary Louise's fiance) dig the rest of the potatoes. Soon the girls were ready to pick up the potatoes for him.

I went to help Samuel, our youngest son, sweep the new 40- x 64-foot machine shed where the ceremony will be held. It was built this summer, and the cement is still easy to clean. Samuel soon left for work as an electrician's helper.

I was not alone long when Albert and the girls were at my heels reporting a fair crop of potatoes, which will help feed the 500 guests that we are expecting to attend the wedding.

William came home with the bench wagon—a boxed-in vehicle which contains enough benches, song books and dishes to be used when church services are held in the home. Then we all joined together in the shed, sweeping, mopping and arranging things to allow lots of needed room.

At 10:30, the fruit man came to bring our order of centerpiece fruit which will be arranged in footed bowls. These bowls will be set on the tables that are set up in all the main rooms in the 

house, with seating for approximately 200 at one time. It's exciting!

This afternoon the laundry was folded, and two more stoves hooked up on L.P. gas. Now we have four stoves to cook on, which will make it handier for the 26 cooks to help prepare the meal of mashed potatoes, chicken gravy, dressing, ham, mixed vegetables, noodles, coleslaw, cheese, celery sticks, cottage cheese and lime Jell-O, prunes, tapioca with bananas and strawberries and pie—cherry, lemon and French apple.

Later, Albert and Mary Louise hitched "Rex" to the buggy and took the cherries, apples, flour and supplies to Grandma's house so she and the girls can bake the pies there on Wednesday.

Also 15 dozen eggs, flour and supplies were sent to a neighbor lady who had offered to help out if needed. Hubby said, "Let her make the noodles if she will." I had been collecting these eggs from our flock of 20 hens.

Earlier today when I went to gather the eggs, "Barney" the stubborn rooster met me at the door. I knew right away that he was in one of his bad moods. I held out my pail, and he fought it. I swung it at him once, twice and the third time he found his corner, only to stand guard until I had gathered the eggs.

At 4 p.m. Samuel came home and helped out in the hog house by vaccinating and moving 100 pigs to make room for the horses to be tied in the barn. With the 83 40-pound pigs we sold Saturday, it should give us plenty of room.

Though I was very tired, I made one more trip to the basement to check if the tables had been properly set and arranged. There is a big "U" table down there and another side table where 64 people can be seated at one time.

I brought back up with me a 5-pound bag of powdered sugar to be used tomorrow to make the frosting for the 26 cakes. Three or four women of the church will come and help bake and frost them. The bottom layer will be chocolate, the middle layer yellow and the top one white.

These cakes will be set on cake stands, one on every table. With the centerpiece fruit, cakes, and glasses of blue, candles and other decorations, we should be well set.

We pray for God's blessings at this special time and ever after.

Jerry Irwin

No Electricity...But They Still Use Refrigerators?

WHENEVER Edna Miller, an Amish farm wife from Ohio who has kept a regular "diary" in *Country* magazine, mentions storing something in her refrigerator, the editors receive letters from readers stating, "But I thought she and other Amish didn't use electricity!"

Edna doesn't, nor do other Old Order Amish families. Edna and they use gas-powered refrigerators, and gas-powered wash machines as well. (Many Amish washing machines have an apparatus that allows a butter churn to be attached to the agitator for making butter.)

Because most refrigerator and washer manufacturers have ceased making the more primitive type of units the Amish depended on, the old units have been mended and rebuilt beyond repair. Finally, Amish housewives have had no choice but to buy more "modern" appliances and adapt them from electric to gas power.

The same approach is becoming increasingly apparent in Amish barnyards and fields, where you will sometimes spot a tractor or mechanical hay baler. Horse-drawn binders, mowers, plows and hay rakes are no longer being turned out by manufacturers, and after mending and rebuilding their original machinery again and again, Amish farmers have been forced to buy what's available.

Still, the tractors are usually not used for pulling but only for belt power or for the power take off which propels corn choppers and silo fillers. The tires may be removed and replaced by steel wheels or steel tires, since pneumatic tires are forbidden by the Old Order Amish.

He Works Up an Appetite as a Carpenter

◆ PROFILE ◆

William and Neoma Coblentz raise miniature horses ("the smaller the better," they say) on their farm located near Sweet Springs. William, a carpenter, works for a local developer framing houses. Still at home are children Lisa, 16, Timothy, 13, Jonathan, 12, and Darlene, 11. William kept this diary.

ACTIVE OUTDOORS. Chores keep them plenty busy, but Coblentz family members take time for outdoor fun too, as evidenced by basketball hoop, trampoline and shuffleboard court in the yard of their Missouri farmhouse.

It is still dark at 5:45 as I head toward the barn to do chores. As I look into the sky, I am reminded of our Sunday School lesson from yesterday, where the Lord told Abraham that his seed will be as the stars of heaven, innumerable. Looks like it will be another beautiful day here in the Midwest. Praise the Lord!

As I walk through the barn, I hear the roosters crow and the horses whinnying. I feed the horses and give water to the chickens. By the time I get back in the house, Neoma is almost finished fixing lunches for me and the schoolchildren.

We sit down to a breakfast of sausage, eggs, homemade bread, grape jelly and cereal. Afterward, Lisa and Darlene do the dishes while Neoma starts with the laundry.

"There's time for chores before supper..."

Married daughter Judy comes over with grandchildren Regina, Melissa, Brian and Nathan. Judy and the boys pick some apples that she wants to use for apple butter and schnitz, "dried apples for half-moon pies".

I go to work where I meet son-in-law Ed. We will be short of help today because Wayne, also a son-in-law, is in Kentucky to visit a brother.

We work on the last of the walls and put up a set of steps in the house we are framing.

For lunch, I have a sandwich with homemade turkey bologna and cheese, potato chips, banana, strawberries, fluffy sponge cake and pecan pie.

This afternoon we put in another set of steps and ceiling joists. We decide to wait for Wayne tomorrow to help put up rafters.

When I come home, there's enough time to do the chores before supper. Tim helps me feed the horses while Jonathan gathers the eggs (14–that's better than the six we got yesterday. Has someone told those hens we've been thinking about chicken stew?).

Neoma has had a busy day. Besides the washing and ironing, she baked a 

DELICIOUS DOINGS. While her husband William works on a home building project, Neoma Coblentz spends the day in the kitchen cooking and baking a hearty supper (above) plus bread, rolls and doughnuts (right).

batch of bread and a cocoa-dot pumpkin cake to take to the sewing circle tomorrow.

For supper we have one of our favorites: taco el plato, homemade bread, jelly, ice tea and homemade ice cream.

This evening Tim, Jonathan and Darlene put straw on the strawberry patch while Lisa helps me dig the last of the sweet potatoes.

Later Lisa writes a letter to a friend and the boys play together upstairs awhile before getting ready to go to bed.

By 9:15, the children are asleep. As I try to finish this up, Neoma tries to do a little reading, but she doesn't get very far. She has probably worked the hardest today.

It's been another wonderful day. Thank you, Lord.

Cleaning, Quilting, Quails Make up This Diarist's Day

◆ PROFILE ◆

Edna Mae Miller lives in a trailer next door to the home of her mother, Fannie, and sister, Betty, near Guthrie, Kentucky. Brother John Jr., his wife, Freida, and their three daughters also live nearby. Edna Mae quilts and does odd jobs for a living besides helping at home.

Shortly before arising at 6 a.m., my usual "getting up" time, I heard coyotes yipping. Although this is no unusual occurrence, it always sets the neighborhood dogs to barking.

It was a beautiful morning, the sky October-clear and a nippy 36°. Fire in the wood heater felt good.

My lone goldfish was fed and watched a bit. I had four until about a month ago, when three died. I'm hoping the next time I go to town I can get some "companions" for him.

After devotions and my favorite breakfast of fried cornmeal mush and scrambled eggs, it was daylight and I was ready to start the day. My pet quails, "Cheeper" and "Bobby", were just "getting up", as they like to wait for daylight before stirring around.

They sleep with me, usually on my pillow against my head, or right beside me. On Mondays they're always grouchy and show it by pecking my feet.

"Misty", our Norwegian Elkhound, was full of energy when I let her loose. We keep her tied at night and when we're gone because we live close to a busy highway. With her company, I brought in more wood and picked the few tomatoes that are still ripening. Our yards and trees are still green due to the ample amount of moisture we've had all summer.

Back inside, I was ready to clean cabinets for fall cleaning. Cheeper and Bobby's curiosity soon won over their "grudge", and they became all involved in watching and checking everything out. When Bobby couldn't see well enough, he'd hop on my shoulder to see from my eye level.

I'm always glad to have them around when I clean. I seldom find roaches, spiders or crickets since I have them, but when I do, they're very glad to eat them.

I didn't do the washing today, as Betty and I take turns to do it and today happened to be her turn. She mopped and waxed their living room floor before leaving for her job at Schlabach's Bakery, where she works 4 days a week.

Mom made peanut brittle—she keeps Schlabach's Bakery supplied during the cooler months. Back in 1959 when I was attending public school, our room had a candy sale to raise money, and Mom donated peanut brittle. People kept asking for more till finally she had a real business of it.

She also weaves rugs to sell when she's able. (Dad made her loom before his death in 1976.) She felt well enough

"My pet quails are always grouchy on Mondays..."

to do some weaving this afternoon. She is afflicted with arthritis and some days hardly feels like working.

Brother John has a veal barn for 268 calves and a chicken house for 11,000-12,000 range-fed broilers. The veal barn was filled Tuesday night with babies from New York, and the chicken house with baby chicks on Thursday. As the calves learn to drink better and the chicks start eating out of the automatic feeders, John and Freida's chores will become easier and less time-consuming. Mom enjoys helping with the calf chores every day, if possible, saying it keeps her going!

I enjoyed my dinner of fried chicken, potatoes in cheese sauce, edible soybeans (my very favorite vegetables), apple salad and a piece of ground cherry pie. The quails hopped up and ate their fill, too.

After a short rest, my clothes were soon folded and put away. They were so sweet-smelling and fluffy. I was glad to finish up my cabinets a short while later. I always like to clean all my cabinets, closets and drawers before starting on the rooms themselves—I think it goes faster!

The next several hours were spent quilting on a red, green and white single Irish chain for a lady from Texas. I quilt only for individuals and do no advertising. Even so, I seem to stay 9 months to a year behind on my waiting list.

The three girls, Rachel, 6, Kathy, 5, and Arlene, 2, came for their daily "visit". They come over for an hour every afternoon, and we usually do whatever they choose. Today I helped them play "kickball" (with Misty watching) and a hiding game in the house.

While they ate a snack, I told them a story out of the book we're in right now, *Touching Incidents and Remarkable Answers to Prayer.* I believe I enjoy these times as much as they do.

This is Rachel's first year in school, and she thoroughly enjoys it. She got a report card today for the first time and was very excited about that. She even brought it along for us to see.

After they left, I ate a quick supper of warmed-up pizza and coleslaw I had put up this summer, then quilted till dark. By then I was ready to work on making net dishrags, which end up in the shape of a ball. I sell lots of these. The quails snuggled down on the couch beside me and watched.

Today was a perfect day, with the temperature climbing into the 70's. The brilliant sunset made me think of a verse we read yesterday in Sunday School. Matthew 16:2 reads: *When it is evening, ye say it will be fair, for the sky is red.*

Before I knew it, 9 was here and time for bed. I like to read awhile after I go to bed, so I turned on the light in the bedroom, then turned off the one in the living room.

The quails came pitter-pattering after me into the bedroom, and we were soon settled in bed, thankful to God for a beautiful and quiet day and asking for His protection through the night.

Sherry Pardee

FINE FOWL. Thousands of range-fed broilers are raised by diarist Edna Mae Miller's brother John, who lives nearby with his wife.

AMISH WEDDINGS have two couples for attendants. Being close friends of the bride and groom, our son Larry and daughter Esther are coupled with the groom's sister and bride's brother for this.

Weddings also include two large meals with about 10 couples as servers, usually boys and girls who are relatives or close friends of the couple. That is how husband Daniel and I met—we served together at the wedding of his uncle and my cousin.

Now our daughter Lorene and her boyfriend Brian will be serving. Of course, it takes cooks, too, so I am one of around 30 women who prepare mashed potatoes, gravy, meat, noodles, dressing, mixed vegetables, cauliflower salad, date pudding, carrot salad, cake, pie and coffee.

After supper, I finished the hand sewing on the dresses. When the bride stopped in for some dishes she needed to borrow, I got those for her and marked them. It takes a lot to cook a meal for 300-plus people, and it all needs to be marked so she knows where it goes afterwards.

—Ruth Miller
Nappanee, Indiana

AFTER SUPPER, the men enjoy an hour or two with their favorite pastime, reading, while I mend socks—a never-ending job, it seems!

Mending socks is getting to be a lost art among lots of the Amish, but I can't bear to throw socks away without putting on a patch or two first like my mother always did.

When they get holes again after being patched, I discard them. I was taught that clothes aren't truly worn out unless patched or mended first.

—Ella Detweiler, Atlantic, Pennsylvania

Who's in Photos? The Shadow Knows!

WHEN we first had the idea for a book written *and* photographed by Amish families, we knew that many Amish adults prefer not to be photographed (see explanation on page 86).

But that doesn't mean Amish folks are unwilling to *take* photographs—in fact, some of them enjoy photography as a hobby.

We offered each of our diarists the opportunity to share photos of their farms, homes, buggies and horses with their diaries, and many accepted. Each was provided with a handy "disposable" camera for this purpose.

Later, as we sorted through the hundreds of photos, we were delighted with the quality...and fascinated by the personal glimpses of Amish family life.

We were also amused to find that, while not many people appeared in the pictures, their *shadows* often did! We couldn't resist including several of them here.

So take a moment to "look over the shoulder" of some friendly Amish photographers!

CONTENTED COWS were snapped in barn doorway by Christ Schlabach, Apple Creek, Ohio.

FARM SCENE at right looked just fine to Christ Miller, Jr. of Millersburg, Ohio.

ROAD HOME (below) was also shot by Christ Miller...recognize his shadow?

CANINE CAPERS were caught on film in snap by David Miller, Millersburg, Oh.

FINE FIELDS of his Jamestown, Pennsylvania farm were overshadowed by Eli Mast.

HORSE AND BUGGY were ready for Dan Hochstetler of Topeka, In.

APPLES were abundant for Andrew Yoder of Oconto, Wisconsin.

MAKING A STAND, playful family pooch posed for Mark Weaver in yard of his Dundee, Ohio farm.

HOME SWEET HOME for Dan Hochstetler and family is this Topeka, In. farm.

Animals of All Sizes Are At Home on this Ohio Farm

◆ PROFILE ◆

Christ and Mary Schlabach farm in Wayne County with son Owen and his wife, Eva, daughter Wilma and her husband, Steve, and sons Marvin, 16, Henry, 13, Reuben, 8, and Steve, 4. In addition to tending fields of barley, corn, hay and oats, the Schlabachs raise broiler chicks, Jersey cows and sows. Christ kept this diary.

The alarm goes off, and with a yawn I realize it must be 4:30 a.m. Marvin, Henry, Reuben and I head for the barn to do our morning chores. This morning we have beautiful clear skies, stars and a 3/4 moon with a temperature of 45°.

We feed our 15 Jersey cows ensilage and a grain mix, which they eat as they're milked by hand. This usually takes about 1-1/2 hours. Henry starts the mechanical cooler and checks the water temperature as well. The milk gets picked up every day and goes to Brewster Dairy for cheese-making.

Next Reuben helps Henry feed our five draft horses, one colt and two road horses. Besides the horses, they feed several dozen calves and heifers. After Marvin does his milking, he tends to six sows, three of which are farrowing now. Then he heads for breakfast and on to work.

"The schoolboys take a short nap after morning chores..."

We all usually make it in to Mom's breakfast table by 7 o'clock for toast, strawberry jam, scrambled eggs, cake and cereals. Then the two schoolboys take a short nap before heading to Maple Grove School with our pony, "Frosty", and their pony cart. She faithfully takes them through any weather on their 1-1/2-mile trip every day.

After breakfast I usually take a stroll down to our 300-foot broiler house. Right now it is empty, but more chicks will arrive this week, and that will certainly fill it with a flurry of activity once more.

Stevie helps me harness up "Barb" and "Kate" to haul sawdust litter for our next batch of chicks. After we get three loads hauled, it's dinnertime.

Finished with her laundry, Mary makes a batch of peanut butter cookies as I go harness up "Bonney" and "Judy" with Barb and Kate. These four horses are my pick to hitch to our Indiana riding plow as I plow silage stalk ground this afternoon.

At 5 o'clock Marvin is home from his job, where he makes lawn furniture. Now we head for supper, which consists tonight of meat loaf, noodles, potatoes, applesauce and upside down date pudding for dessert.

After supper we head for the barn to do evening chores and then chat with a neighbor that stops by. The rest of the evening is spent reading while Marvin and Henry play Ping-Pong.

A BIG GARDEN just outside the back door of the Schlabachs' farmhouse is neatly fenced in.

BABY CHICKS quickly learn to use the feeders and waterers inside spacious broiler house.

PLENTY OF PUMPKINS plus some pleasing flowers and shrubs line the walk and steps that lead from the farmhouse up to the barn.

GROWING BOYS. The Belgian colt with one of the Schlabach boys above is just learning the ropes while team below is hauling grain.

Why Does Amish Schooling End with the Eighth Grade?

THE AMISH believe that too much education makes children too "worldly", and that public high schools include courses that the Amish child will likely never use.

Why teach science to a boy who will devote his life to farming? Why teach chemistry to a girl who will become a housewife and mother?

This philosophy ran straight in the face of what the government felt *all* children should be taught, and for years the Amish faced legal pressure and even occasional imprisonment. Finally, the Supreme Court decided that religious freedom ranked ahead of educational requirements and exempted Amish children from compulsory attendance beyond the eighth grade.

The Amish feel that 4 years of high school would deprive their children of some of their most valuable learning years. It's during these teenage years that the boys are in the fields and barns working with their fathers, and the girls are helping out in the homes with their mothers.

Still, the Amish feel that some early, formal education is important, and this is usually given in one of the numerous one-room schoolhouses still scattered through Amish areas (numerous so Amish children are within walking distance).

These schools are built and maintained by the Amish (with no tax funds), and they print their own textbooks. The teacher is usually an Amish woman who likewise has no more than an eighth grade education, and whose aim is to teach basic *values*, not basic skills.

This distinction was made by Chief Justice Warren Berger of the Supreme Court in 1972 when he ruled that "It is neither fair nor correct to suggest that the Amish are opposed to education beyond the eight grade level. What the record shows is that they are opposed to conventional formal education of the type provided by certified high schools because it comes at the child's crucial adolescent period of religious development."

Ronald Wilson

Two Families Share Crops, Cows, Horses

Cheery greetings from south-central Iowa! It was a gorgeous morning—the sunshine glistening on trees only beginning to show their autumn colors made a beautiful sight!

While the rest of the family began morning chores which consist of milking our dairy cows by hand and feeding the horses, sister Lavina and I started with housework.

First on the list was fixing a lunch for our brother Thomas to eat at the school he teaches, and preparing an early breakfast for him.

Sunrise Ridge School is located 4 miles away. On a day like this, using his spirited horse "Jerry", the drive is anything but unpleasant.

Enrollment is 17 pupils from grades one through eight. All of the families in our settlement moved here from other areas, so the curriculum is new to everyone. This, in turn is challenging for Thomas to see to the needs of each student.

Once chores were finished, I treated the family to a favorite breakfast of pancakes served with homemade syrup, eggs, graham cereal, glad times cake, homemade bread and mint tea we raised.

Using eight of our Belgians, Dad and brothers Paul and Mose headed for the fields. Dad drove the corn binder while the boys shocked the corn once it was cut. Later it will be shredded, and we will use the stalks for bedding.

One of the cows had gone bad, so we arranged for a neighbor to pick it up tomorrow to sell at the sale barn in Humeston. Mose also plans to send a few hogs along.

Mother did the laundry this morning. With a gentle breeze and a temperature of 70°, it dried quickly.

As I resumed my day's duties, my thoughts returned to the happenings of yesterday. After a restful Sunday at home, we drove 11 miles to Eli Yoder's (a 52-minute drive via horse and buggy) for supper and, afterwards, singing German hymns.

These songs, written hundreds of years ago, seem to have greater depth and meaning than many of the modern-day ones.

The beautiful moonlit eve, perfect for driving, was marred only by a passing motorist who almost rammed into us. Another car was coming from the opposite direction while we were in the midst of the conflict, almost forcing us into the ditch. Thankfully, we escaped serious injuries.

◆ PROFILE ◆

Lydia Helmuth lives with her parents, two brothers (Paul and Thomas) and a sister (Lavina) on a 160-acre farm that straddles Lucas and Wayne counties. The house is in Wayne and the barn and garden are in Lucas. Another brother, Mose, and his family live on a nearby 120-acre farm which is also owned by the parents. Everyone pitches in to tend 23 cows and 18 horses, plus 4 horses at Mose's farm.

Mark Weaver

Maynard Knepp

TWO-COUNTY COWS. Since their Iowa farm straddles two counties, the Helmuths' cows and calves might graze in one, milk in another.

This afternoon Lavina was busily mowing the lawn, using our push mower. This is quite an accomplishment for a "special" girl. In her spare time, she's teaching "Chirpy Blue", her newly acquired parakeet, to talk.

Most of my afternoon was taken up baking nut and pumpkin pies, cleaning Sunday clothes by hand and preparing the noon meal.

Lunch consisted of escalloped potatoes, beans and carrots from the garden, hamburger and a vegetable salad. There was sweetheart pudding, chocolate oatmeal cookies and pumpkin pie for dessert.

After the laundry was done, Mother decided to paint new wheels for the buggy. The old ones just might collapse at a time when we don't want them to!

Later, after the ironing was finished, I started another quilt project. This time, instead of a wall hanging, my goal is a queen-sized tumbling block pattern in Christmas colors.

Now that harvesting has begun, work on the barn we're building has slowed considerably. A silo foundation has been cemented now. Three barns have been or are being raised among the Amish of this settlement (seven families total), plus two silos, parts of three houses and various other smaller buildings.

We heard by mail today of visitors planning a stopover in Iowa. The group is mainly Mother's cousins from North Carolina, Ohio and Pennsylvania. Also included is an aunt, 88 years old, coming to visit Grandma, 92, and Grandpa, also 92.

Evening arrived, and Thomas returned home from school. He'd planned a PTA meeting for tomorrow night.

In the distance, we could hear the yipping of the coyotes. I, for one, was ready to retire after a day crammed with activities.

CHAPTER FOUR

Applique and pieced quilt top, cotton,
"Friendship Quilt" pattern, possibly made by Lydia A. Bradley in
Drumore township, Lancaster County, c. 1845-1875

IN TOUCH with their crops and animals, most Amish farmers depend on horsepower and manpower at chore time. Smaller spreads and plenty of personal attention mean quality crops.

Jon Paris

Friends, Family Help Out Following a House Fire

◆ PROFILE ◆

Lester and Edna Bontranger raise cattle on their small farm in LaGrange County. Of their four children, two are at home: Orville, 29, and Calvin, 25. Lester and Calvin work at Star Craft Camper company in Topeka, Indiana where they make fifth-wheel trailers. Edna stays at home and cares for Orville, who is bedridden. Two days before Edna wrote this diary, the Bontrangers had a severe house fire.

First my prayer for today is for help and strength from our good Lord, who giveth and who taketh away again.

Today is a day like we never went through before and would not hope to afterward. I got up at 2:30 a.m. and started cleaning inside and out. We had a house fire Saturday evening, which did serious damage.

The fire started from a gas floor lamp and was out of control in minutes. The first thing we did was get our invalid 29-year-old son, Orville, out.

Lester used the fire extinguisher, but it was too big a fire already, as gas was shooting out of the lamp. He ran and called the 911 number, then took Orville over to the neighbor's across the street. Calvin, our other son, was not at home till it was all over with.

This morning at 4:30, Lester and Calvin got up and started first with fixing the Kero water heater, which got shut off from the fire. We have two houses together with a washhouse in between. The other house was also filled with smoke during the fire, but we got that cleaned enough to stay in over the weekend.

At 5 we had breakfast of sausages and eggs. By then Orville was awake and wanting his breakfast of oatmeal, so I fed him and got him changed and all cleaned up.

Next, the menfolk put our washing machine out in the yard, and I started washing at 5:30. Everything in our house that we could save needed to be washed.

Around 8, the neighbor ladies started to come and help clean up. All the dishes are black and had to be soaked, scrubbed and washed. A few menfolk helped carry out the stove, refrigerator and other kitchen furniture. Then some washed walls, others windows and floors.

It was a nice, sunshiny day, and the wash dried fast out on the line. When noontime came, we had our lunch of meat and vegetables, salad and lots of desserts, which was all brought in from the kind ladies who came to help today.

In the afternoon, most of us were scrubbing and washing dishes. Some kept on bringing wash in from the line and helped fold, and I tried to find a place to put it, as we lost all of our living furniture. The bedroom furniture could be saved, but needs to be washed and scrubbed.

Our two married sons came in the evening and helped carry in the stoves and bedroom set. They stayed for supper, which was leftovers from noon.

By 8, everyone was very tired and ready for bed. The neighbor ladies each took wash along home yet to wash tomorrow.

After a prayer of thanks for kind people and friends, and the things we still have that were not burned, and that no one was hurt, we went to bed.

I want to share this yet: When the bookcase full of books was brought out of the house after the fire, a small Bible was open at Timothy.

What touched us was verse 7, which reads, *You have brought nothing into this world, and it is certain we can carry nothing out again. And, having food and raiment, let us therefore be content.*

❖ Why Do Amish Hold Church Services in Their Homes? ❖

IN MOST Amish communities, church services are held in a different Amish home each week. The church "bench wagon"—which resembles a horse-drawn hearse—brings a number of hard, backless benches or chairs the day before or the morning of services.

Then a dozen or more families will gather at the home on Sunday morning, some coming by buggy up to 10 miles or more. The service usually lasts at least 4 hours and is followed by a lunch.

This practice of moving the service from home to home actually began in Switzerland way back in the early 1500's, when the church and state there were trying to wipe out this new faith. So the Amish were forced—both for personal and religious reasons—to meet "secretly" for worship.

They began meeting in their homes, selecting a different home each week so that it appeared as though they were "visiting". That practice has carried over to this day, even though there is no longer any need for secrecy.

While the Amish now enjoy religious freedom here, they seem determined never to forget the years of persecution that finally drove them from their native land.

For private reading, there are three books that will be found in every Old Order Amish home—the Bible, the *Ausbund* (a Protestant hymnal), and *The Martyr's Mirror* (nearly 1,000 pages long, it chronicles the suffering and harassment endured by the founders of their faith).

Farmhouse Addition Will Soon Add Welcome Space

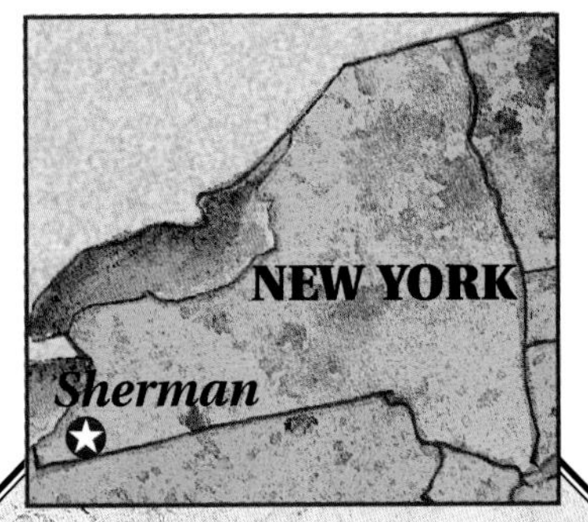

◆ PROFILE ◆

Andy and Fannie Miller's scenic Sherman, New York, dairy farm is just a 10-minute drive from world-famous Chautauqua Lake. On their 190 acres they grow their own feed of oats, corn, hay and silage, doing their farming with horses. Three of the Millers' ten children still live at home: Sylvia and her husband, Andy, Arlene, 25, and John Andrew, 18. Fannie kept this diary.

The alarm went off at 5 as usual, and soon we were started with the milking. We milk by hand with help from daughter Sylvia, her husband, Andy, and their four lively little boys, who recently moved in with us.

Husband Andy and I are living in our front hall until our 20- x 40-foot kitchen and living room addition and remodeled bedroom and bath are finished. The men are doing the work themselves, so it's slow going.

After a breakfast of eggs, homemade bread and cereal, I started the washing. "My" Andy fed the calves and cleaned the barn and milk house, and son-in-law Andy left for his job at the sawmill in Sherman. Arlene left at 7 for her teaching job—this is her 6th year.

Later, Andy took down a fence to move to another field while John split and stacked firewood. Since the men finished filling silo last week, they have been getting other necessary jobs done before winter (and deer season).

Our oldest daughter Mary Alice came by with two of her little girls for me to watch while she took the two youngest for shots. She brought some fresh venison steaks from an 8-point buck her husband Marvin shot with bow and arrow in Pennsylvania (we're only 10 miles from the state line).

Laundry was finished soon after 10, so I kept Sylvia's baby (9 months old) while she did hers. I swept out our living quarters and mixed a big batch of chocolate chip cookies, hoping to bake them before lunch. The peanut butter cookies and turtle cake I made Saturday had all disappeared.

Jonas Coblentz

WOODPILE is used year-round for cooking, heating and warming up the wash water.

I had many interruptions. First a potato salesman stopped in, then our faithful producer of most of our canning fruit with some Cortland apples. They are extra nice and big this year.

Then someone came to look at our wood burning kitchen range, which is for sale. (Our remodeled kitchen will have an airtight wood burning kitchen range that will hold a fire overnight.)

There was only time for a thrown-together lunch of grilled cheese and tomato sandwiches, milk, leftover potato salad and leftover cake.

It started sprinkling right after lunch, so I quickly brought in my wash while cookies were baking. It had been hard to hang up and keep wash on the line this morning with a strong wind, but the clothes were oh-so soft and fluffy.

After lunch, Andy and John hitched up two of our Belgian draft horses to a wagon and took fence posts and wire to put up fence in another field for the cows. All the rain we've been having

❖ Do the Amish Pay Taxes? ❖

YES they do, and school taxes are particularly hard to bear for them, since the Amish educate their own children, build and maintain their own school buildings and provide their own teachers and textbooks.

Still, they pay school taxes for children other than their own. And, as more "English" families move away from big cities and settle on the edges of Amish communities, the increased need for more public schools further increases the tax burden for the Amish.

David Miller

AMISH SCHOOLS are built and maintained with private funds, not taxes paid by the Amish.

has kept everything lush and green.

I washed dishes and picked late green beans and a few cucumbers in the garden. It started raining at 4, so I helped Sylvia bring her wash in, then watched her baby while she did lots of phoning around to find some grapes to can into juice and jelly.

As it was raining and the men could not work on the addition this evening, Sylvia and her family went to visit Andy's folks as soon as he came home from work at 6.

Arlene came home at 4 and made out a library book order for her scholars before helping with the milking.

Supper was fresh venison steaks, mashed potatoes, gravy, fresh green beans and vegetable pizza. Just as we finished, daughter Betsie, her husband, Marvin, and their three little ones came over, along with several friends and neighbors, with ice cream and chips for a birthday surprise for Andy and me (both our birthdays were last week) We enjoyed a nice visit.

Soon after our company left, we headed for bed, knowing the rest of the week would be just as busy and full as today was. Church will be here again on Sunday—the third time!

Good night, and God bless each and every one of you.

Visitors Fill Their Home with Happiness

◆ PROFILE ◆

Herman and Lydia Stutzman grow oats, corn, hay and wheat and raise some 300 hogs on their 115-acre farm in Clare County. They have three milk cows for family use, plus their neighbors supply them with milk as needed. The Stutzmans have eight children: Joseph, 26, Herman Jay, 22, Mary Ann, 24, Jerry Roy, 21, Martha Fern, 17, Samuel, 15, Barbara Sue, 11 and Nelson, 9. Lydia kept this diary.

WELCOME HOME. Without autos for transportation, visitors from out of town are rare but welcome at Stutzmans' home (above). At right: Windmill pump provides well water for livestock.

Our day usually starts at 5:45, but this morning I never heard the alarm, and it was almost 6 when I woke.

Fresh water was put on for coffee, and the bacon in the pan for breakfast. Instead of my usual calling to wake the children upstairs, I took the broom handle and tapped on the kitchen ceiling to wake the girls, so as not to waken our visitors—Herman's nephew, Joe Yoder, wife Velma and baby Aaron, 4 months, here from Missouri for the weekend.

The girls were soon down. Martha fixed Samuel's dinner bucket while Barbara fixed her and Nelson's school lunches. Herman went out to do some of the chores before breakfast.

Son Jerry soon got up, grabbed a few pieces of bacon and his bow to get in a few hours of hunting before going to work.

I then called the rest of the family for breakfast, plus our visitors. We were all at the table by 7. Breakfast was bacon and eggs, warm raisin bread, cereal, frozen blueberries and coffee. After breakfast, we had our morning devotions as usual.

It was 42°, cloudy and chilly, with a good breeze blowing, so we got a fire started in the heating stove. It was soon more cozy in here.

After breakfast, the men went to finish chores. Martha washed the dishes while nephew Joe dried them. Baby Aaron was given his bath while I cleaned up a bit from yesterday's houseful of company.

Took the extra leafs out of the table, which had been spread out 14 feet as our two married children, Jay and Mary Ann, were home for dinner to visit with 

Joe. Five other families came yesterday to visit with them, as well. It was too far to go visit each family in one day with the horse, so we had invited them all here instead.

We popped two 20-quart bowls of popcorn and made 4 gallons of drink for a snack.

Just before 8, Samuel grabbed his lunch bucket and left for his job at the mill just 1/2 mile up the road. At 8:15, Barbara and Nelson biked the 2 miles to school. Herman hitched "Knight", our standardbred, to our buggy so I could take Joe and Velma to visit another cousin, then make a stop at our school for a brief visit.

We arrived at school in time to enjoy their morning songs and listen to their new Bible verses for the week, plus enjoy a class of math before Joe's driver came to pick them up for their journey farther south. They wanted to be in Indiana for the night.

It was 10 when I came home with the buggy. Daughter Martha had also left to help a neighbor for the day with some extra work, and Herman left around 9 for his usual job at the stockyards, where he works only on Mondays.

Joseph didn't need to go to his job today, so I "sweet-talked" him into churning butter for me. After doing that, he started the motor and, using our pressure washer, cleaned our buggy inside and out before taking it to the repair shop.

Several weeks ago, one of the boys forgot to fasten one line to the bridle while hitching "Knight" to our buggy. The result was a badly damaged buggy when Knight kept going around in circles and the buggy was thrown on its side, breaking different parts. We could still use it, though it looked very lopsided. The shop couldn't repair it till this week.

"I sweet-talked Joseph into churning butter..."

After I changed into my everyday clothes, I cut a vest for a neighbor boy who needs a new one for his sister's wedding on Thursday. By the time I was done cutting, it was lunchtime. Joseph and I had a bowl of vegetable soup, hot chocolate and watermelon.

This afternoon, a neighbor brought four teams and wagons to haul around 400 bales of green baled hay. We didn't need the third cutting alfalfa ourselves, so we sold it to another farmer, who baled it Saturday. Later, our friends

READY WHEELS. Like most Amish families, the Stutzmans have a variety of buggies and wagons—some open and some enclosed—for transporting personal belongings and family members.

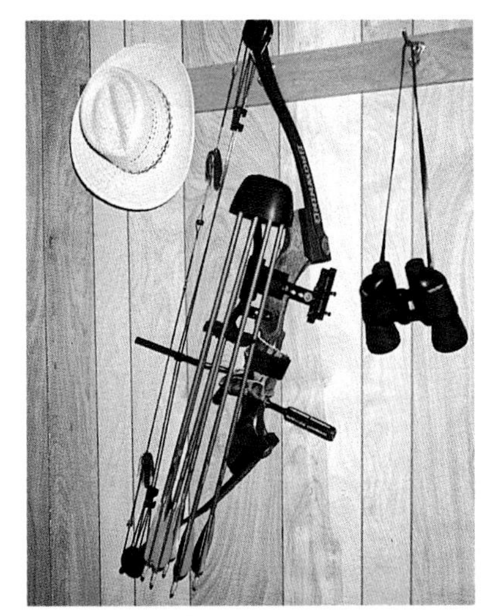

PIGS APLENTY fill the farrowing house year-round on this Michigan farm (above), and three cows provide milk for growing children. At right: Son Jerry's bow hunting gear awaits after chores.

COZY QUARTERS. Warmth of wood paneling, thick bedspread make this bedroom comfortable.

from Midland, Ken and Carol, with their grandson Lance, brought us several boxes of papers, which we shred and use as bedding for the pigs. Lance enjoys visiting the farm and also jumping on the trampoline in the backyard.

Barbara and Nelson arrived home from school at 3:35. They changed into chore clothes and, after a snack, went to pick some wild grapes growing along the road by our property (we love the wild grape jelly). Then they started chores, feeding the calves, rabbits, chickens, and keeping the water troughs filled.

Samuel came home from work soon after 5. He needed to fill some hog feeders and milk the family cow. I got supper in the oven.

We had so many leftovers from yesterday that I fixed a casserole of meat loaf, a layer of mashed potatoes and gravy on top. Also made sweet corn and plate salad, plus blueberries and ice cream for dessert. We ate supper at 6:30.

Barbara and Nelson went to bring in the butternut squash from the garden while Martha and I did dishes. The rest relaxed with a book till bedtime.

By 9:30, we were ready to call it a day. Just as we headed to bed, son Jerry came home. "Your supper's in the oven," I told him. "Good night."

And God's blessings to each and everyone.

Ronald N. Wilson

WE HAVE two sorrel Belgian workhorses, "May" and "Minnie". Our faithful driving horse, "Diane" (we call her Di for short), is 16 years old. I dread to think when we can't use her anymore. Our first driving horse got to be 21 years old. Hubby Joe is very easy and kind to horses. I always feel sorry for animals with rough masters.

Our dog, "Lucky", we found on the church house steps one night as we were going up to visit one of our married daughters. Someone had dumped the poor puppy off. Son Alvin went and got him, and he sat beside us on the buggy seat all the way home. *—Sylvia Stutzman*
Columbia, Kentucky

Amish Pay Their Respects

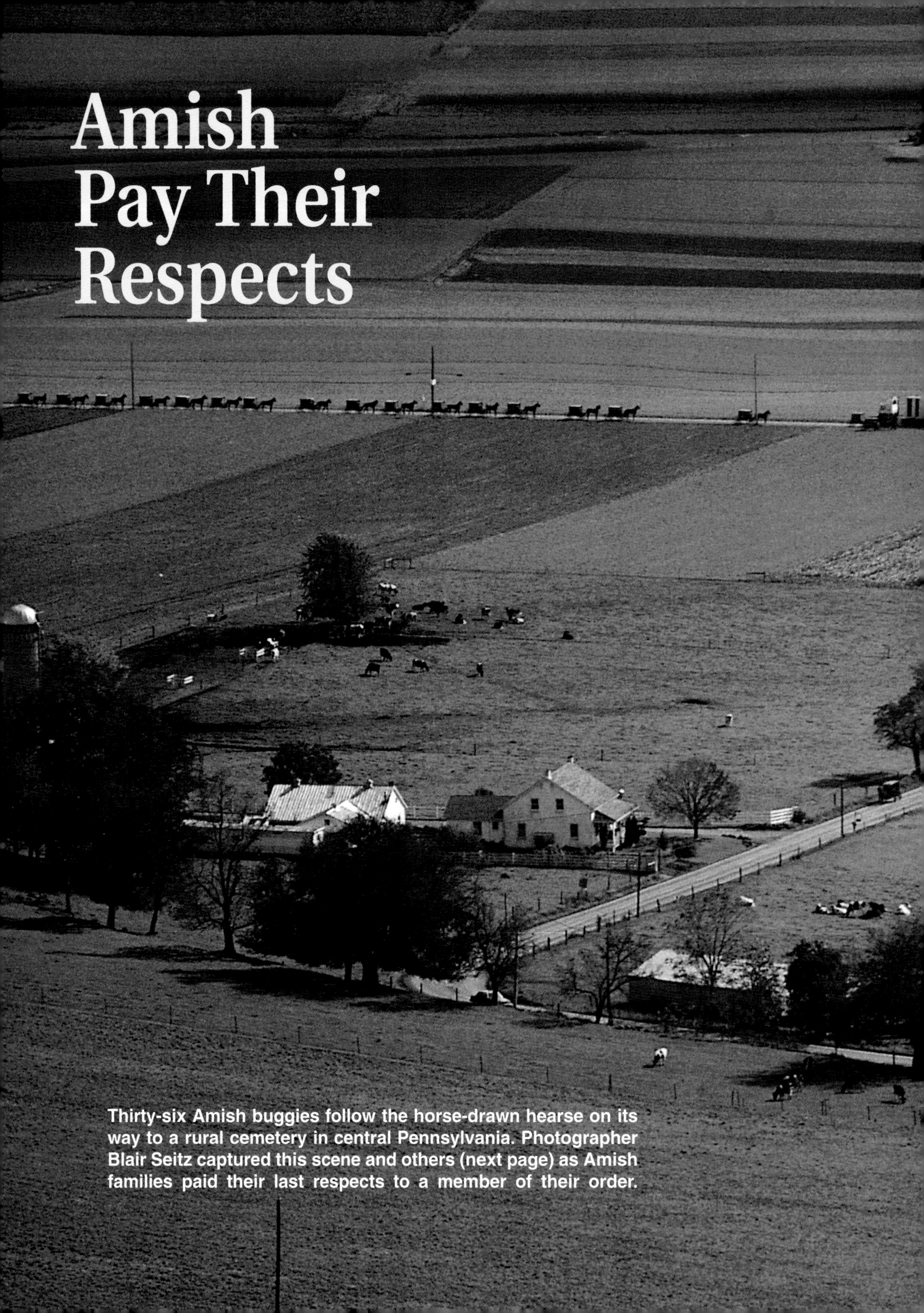

Thirty-six Amish buggies follow the horse-drawn hearse on its way to a rural cemetery in central Pennsylvania. Photographer Blair Seitz captured this scene and others (next page) as Amish families paid their last respects to a member of their order.

A HIGHWAY PATROLMAN (at top of left photo) regulates traffic as Amish buggies follow hearse to cemetery situated among Amish farmlands (at right). Church and family members perform many of the services that funeral directors normally perform for non-Amish families. After embalming, the body is returned home for viewing. The funeral service is held at the home, attended by many friends and relatives. They gather again at the cemetery (below left) to once more view the body in the open air, and participate in a simple service. A plain, granite marker is placed at the head of the grave. After the service, immediate family members (below) respectfully remain at the grave site until the earth is mounded over the opening.

Photos from *Amish Country* by Ruth and Blair Seitz, Harrisburg, Pennsylvania

Busy Brother and Sister Find Time to go Fishing

◆ PROFILE ◆

Susie Beachy, 76, and her brother Mahlon, 62, live on the 120-acre farm near Garnett settled by their parents back in 1915. Relatives now tend to the farming, but Susie and Mahlon still remain active. Mahlon tends 11 hives of bees and extracts the honey in summertime, and Susie cans vegetables from her big garden. Both love to fish from their boat on the creek which runs through their woodland. Susie kept this diary.

This morning brother Mahlon and I arose at 5:30 to a beautiful sunshiny day with temperature at 50°. For our breakfast we ate fried cornmeal mush and tomato gravy, a favorite of many Amish.

Then Mahlon fed our brown standardbred driving horse, "Lew", and went down the road 1/4 mile on his bicycle to feed grain to some young cattle which our brother-in-law and nephew have grazing in our pastureland.

After doing the breakfast dishes and making beds, I got busy peeling Golden Delicious apples which grew in our orchard this summer and canned several quarts of applesauce. Have done 60 quarts so far this fall and a few more to go later.

After I was finished with the applesauce, I went to the garden and pulled some radishes (fall planting), also cut off the okra. The garden is about done, but the okra stalks are still blooming. Tomorrow I'll cut up the okra and fry it for breakfast with scramble eggs over it and also fix tomato gravy to go with it.

After doing his chores, Mahlon hauled a load of wood which he sawed up in our woodland on Saturday to Garnett for a customer. This was mostly oak and ash wood. I sent our laundry along with him to the laundromat to have it done, and I hung it out after he got home before dinner yet.

> *"Caught three nice-sized bass, about 3/4 pound each..."*

For dinner I fixed chicken and noodles using canned chicken from the cellar, plus green beans and slaw.

Later this afternoon Mahlon went to our woods and sawed up another load for the same customer. After getting home about evening, he put the blade on the tractor and smoothed up around the barnyard where there were some mud holes in preparation for a trucker to bring crushed rock to put here and there around some of the buildings around here. He put in a full day.

This afternoon I got the laundry in from the clothesline and folded it. Next I peeled and cut up my small sweet potatoes I had dug along with the bigger ones last week. I cold-pack them in pint jars in the pressure cooker. The larger sweet potatoes I wrap in paper, put in cardboard boxes and store upstairs in a cool room for the winter. They will keep till spring.

Later I got several jars of honey, put some nice sweet potatoes in paper bags, also cut several heads of cockscomb from the garden, ready to all be taken to the community sale in the morning to be sold. These all sell well.

Weatherwise, it was a gorgeous day—by afternoon it got as warm as 80° with a good breeze. Farmers were busy on this day combining soybeans, corn and milo maize, all good crops.

No frost yet, so flowers are still blooming so pretty. Even the Robin Hood roses are still blooming. The trees are beginning to change color and are so pretty. With our ample rainfall all summer, the grass is nice and green.

I decided after a busy day to give myself a treat. Soon after 4 p.m. I walked across the road to our pond, which is stocked with fish, and fished for an hour or two. Caught three nice-sized bass, perhaps weighing about 3/4-pound each. Yummy!

By the time it was dark, we called it a day.

WHILE WAITING on supper, I worked on a shirt for Andy to wear to school. It had been a Sunday shirt the older boys grew out of, so I cut it down for Andy. That reminded me of this poem:

Stretching a Dollar

They tell me you work for a dollar a day;
How is it you clothe six boys on such pay?
I know you think it conceited and queer,
But I do it because I'm a good financier.
There's Pete, John, Jim, Joe, Bill and Ed—
A half-dozen boys to be clothed and fed.
And I buy for them all, good plain victuals to eat.
But clothing—I buy only clothing for Pete.
When Pete's clothes are too small for him to get on,
My wife makes them over and gives them to John.
When for John, who is 10, they have grown out-of-date,
She makes them over for Joe, who is 8.
And when little Joe can wear them no more,
She makes them over for Bill, who is 4.
And when for young Bill they no longer will do,
She still makes them over for Ed, who is 2.
So you see if I get enough clothing for Pete,
The family is furnished with a wardrobe complete.
But when Ed gets through with the clothing
And you'd call them wore out, what do we do then?
Why once more we go around the circle complete
And begin to use them for patches for Pete!

—Lydia Miller, Fredericksburg, Ohio

Folks from All Over Enjoy the Meals Here

Good morning. Lord, you are usher of another new day, untouched and freshly new. So here I come to ask you, God, that you'll renew me, too.

5 o'clock and time to get up. Andy and I have our cup of coffee to start off a good day. We usually chat about half an hour before waking Linda and Betty. It's now 15 till 6, and the girls are trying to wake up.

Breakfast is ready: ham, eggs and cold cereal. Then Andy goes off to the sawmill while Linda milks the cow (a Jersey) and feeds the calves. At the same time, Betty sets the tables for 46 people from Canada who'll be coming later on a tour bus. I start to bake bread and pies.

LOADS OF LAUNDRY are washed and hung on the line behind Rabers' home between loads of tourists who come there to eat.

◆ **PROFILE** ◆

Andy and Maudie Raber live on an 80-acre farm near Millersburg. Andy runs a sawmill, and Maudie cooks and bakes for the many tourists that visit the area. Of their eight children, daughters Betty and Linda still live at home. Maudie kept this diary.

Now our guests are here. Today's menu is broccoli with cheese soup or chicken and noodle soup, a big tossed salad and a variety of pies. They are tickled with the pies—fresh peach, coconut cream, ground cherry, custard and black raspberry. A lot of them eat two pieces—a good sign!

"We set tables for 46 Canadian guests..."

After the tourists leave, the girls and I eat our dinner. Daughter Marie drops in and helps us clean up and reset the tables for another bus group to-

A CUT ABOVE. As Andy became busier with his sawmill business, the family sold their small dairy herd and stopped raising broilers as well.

BOARDS FOR BUILDING stack up outside sawmill, which employs six men. When one has a day off, daughter Betty Raber takes his place.

morrow. Marie lives at the back end of our farm and is one of my extra cooks when we need more help. Her three girls, ages 6, 4 and 1, are my *future* cooks. Ha!

Linda decides we should do the laundry yet since we have a bus to cook for every day this week. So she does that

"A lot of our guests eat two pieces of pie —a good sign!"

while Betty and I work on baking more bread and cooking pie filling for tomorrow's pies.

Tomorrow's menu will be chicken and ham, mashed potatoes, dressing, gravy, noodles, corn, coleslaw, homemade bread, pie, coffee and tea. Anybody hungry? Stop in and help us eat the leftovers!

GONE FISHIN'. While adults enjoy an Amish-style meal, these two tykes try their luck at lake.

WELL-STOCKED PANTRY provides Maudie and her helpers with plenty of ingredients for making plump pies and luscious loaves (right).

DINING HALL fills up fast when busloads of tourists arrive at the Raber farm almost daily during summer. Right: Hungry tourists fill up, too!

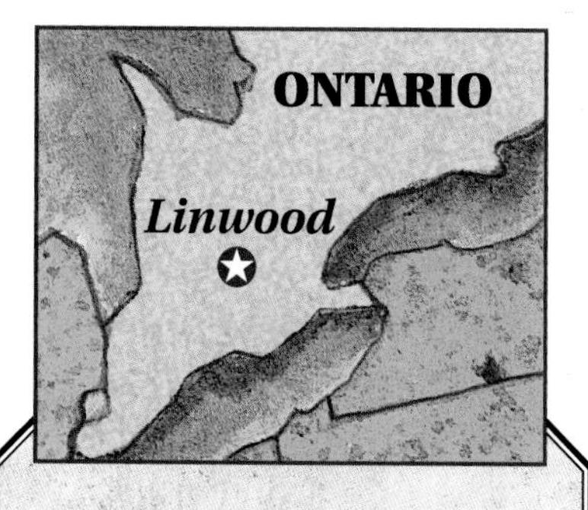

Machine Shop, Grain Crop Top Their Days in Canada

◆ PROFILE ◆

Elmer and Leah Kuepfer grow corn, wheat, mixed grains and hay on their farm near Linwood. In addition, they run a machinery service and supply shop. Four grown daughters still at home: Ruthann, Verna, Marilyn and Christena. Elmer kept this diary.

As usual this morning at 5 a.m., the alarm clock loudly insists on some attention. After pushing down the button, I catch another 60 quick winks, one for each year.

Ten minutes later, I light the old Coleman lamp and pull my chair up to my desk for the early morning hours—the best ones for some uninterrupted catching up of the mail and the bills.

With the arrival of daylight, the east shows promise of sunrise soon. A verse comes to mind: *Truly the light is sweet, and a pleasant thing it is for the eyes to behold the sun* (Ecclesiastes 11, verse 7). However, it turns out that we do not get to see the sun until late afternoon.

Presently, we have most of our barn rented out. Part of it is rented to nephew Lloyd Zehr, who raises meat rabbits commercially. Son-in-law Allan Albrecht, eldest daughter Melinda's husband, also rents barn space for market hogs. That leaves us with only our horses to tend, so morning chores are soon finished.

Breakfast at 6:30 is fried eggs with ham and cheese and several choices of cereal. I pour some homemade granola-type cereal with nuts because I like it...then I cover it with All-Bran because wife Leah (usually referred to as "Mom") says it is good for me. I slice half of a ripe banana to top it off.

Presently, as part of our morning devotions, we use an old hymnbook first printed nearly 100 years ago. It contains old favorite English hymns translated into German. This morning's selection is the German version of *Blessed Assurance*.

Next I help daughter Verna, a teacher, hitch "Prince" to the buggy. (Our other standardbred is called "Surge", short for his registered name, "Plastic Surgeon". He's reliable, safe and steady, so Mom and the girls can get him into overdrive when they consider it necessary.) Soon Verna leaves to pick up Rosemary Albrecht, who is her co-teacher at Amish Parochial School No. 1.

Meanwhile, Mom is busy canning grapes, and daughter Marilyn can be heard down in the cellar singing to the accompaniment of the little Honda gasoline engine on the Maytag wringer washer.

Daughter Ruthann leaves to help at Allan's, and youngest daughter Christena goes to help our other married daughter, Norma, wife of Amos Albrecht. We are very fortunate to have our two married daughters within a mile of home.

James Jantzi, who has been our right-hand man for nearly 12 years now, arrives to work in the shop. His main work today will be to rebuild Paul Kuepfer's 7 HP Lister diesel engine, used to power the milking machine and water pump at Paul's farm.

My first customer at the counter is an "English" lady looking for a part for her Maytag wringer washer so she doesn't have to wring the rest of her wash by hand.

The morning is soon gone as I wait on customers and repair a few Coleman lanterns for those who say that the time has come to get their lamps and lanterns in good shape as daylight hours are growing shorter.

Dinner at 12 consists of mashed potatoes and burger patties with cheddar cheese, steamed carrots and cauliflower prepared with browned butter and apple dumplings for dessert.

This afternoon nephew Ezra Kuepfer comes to work, so I help him bring our Belgians, "Jeanie" and "Bessie", from pasture. Jeanie is acting a bit contrary today, so our dog "Twinkles" also lends a hand.

We have a decision to make. Shall we pick stones off the fall wheat, which is already 2-3 inches high...or shall we plow the garden? Well, with Mom busy elsewhere, it is easier to make the decision—picking up stones it is.

Christena is back from Amoses, so she and Marilyn do final cleanup in the garden and attend to their Country Footwear, Lamp and Clock Shop here in our yard. It is owned and operated by our four younger daughters who still call this "home".

By late afternoon it is colder yet sunny, and the wind has gone down. There will be a hard frost tonight like the one last week, which brought an end to Mom's raspberry crop that had been producing exceptionally well.

I keep busy in the shop preparing our wood-burning boiler for the coming heating season. Four grandsons and one granddaughter walk by here on their way home from school, and they stop in and visit for a while.

Good! There goes the supper bell. I clean up and go to the house, only to find it's a false alarm—there is still half an hour to go. I learn that grandson Elmer was the trickster, and he left hurriedly for home.

Finally, supper is ready—a thick homemade vegetable and turkey soup, with fresh grape pie for dessert. Afterward I go back to the shop for a while and then do a bit of outside work until dark.

Back in the house I am writing this diary when granddaughter Muriel, age 4, sees her chance to pester Grandpa. She pulls up a chair, clamps her arms around my neck and climbs up on my back.

By the time the grandchildren are put to bed and we are settled and the lights are out, the alarm clock reminds us of its presence with an eerie glow; we see that it is 9:30 p.m. Good night!

Visits from the Grandkids Bring Sunshine to the Day

◆ PROFILE ◆

Levi and Naomi Esh have a shoe store and shoe repair shop tucked between three adjoining farms where three sons-in-law grow corn and hay and milk 45 cows. The Eshes have been blessed with 11 grandchildren ranging in age from 3 weeks to 10 years. Levi kept this diary.

It is a clear, 38° morning as I head for the barn to feed our two driving horses and the pony. The dozen laying hens need a scoopful of feed as well.

Meantime, Mom (wife Naomi) runs the iron kettle full of water for the Monday wash. I gather some kindling in the woods to start the fire under the kettle and also to revive the dying fire in the kitchen wood stove.

Finally I'm getting around to fixing the broken hinge on Mom's gas range. For the past 4 weeks we've been into the busiest season of the year—silo-filling—and spare moments were few. Breakfast will be at 7, so I have enough time to grab the toolbox in the shop and change a broken roller on the oven door hinge.

There are four of us at the breakfast table: Mom, son Emanuel, age 20, daughter Ruth, age 17, and me. On the menu this morning are omelets with green peppers and onions, bacon, coffee and shoe-fly pie. There is also a large bowl of concord grapes to pick away on for our fruit.

Following breakfast, Emanuel and I head for the shoe shop. Emanuel is the repairman, and there are shoes and boots stacked everywhere awaiting repairs. I need to check order sheets and call in reorders this morning.

At 8 o'clock our good neighbor Lee Snyder stops in for his daily visit. Lee worked at Harrisburg in the steel mill for 20-some years until doctors put him on disability after heart surgery.

Now he travels the valley early every morning in his Ford pickup to see what's going. He's at the coffee shop at 5:30, then around to several other stops before stopping here to see if we need anything in town or need any equipment parts from over the mountain.

This morning we load up several bushels of acorns that Ruth had raked up in the yard last week. Lee drops off the acorns with Elam Lapp, who has a small herd of white-tailed deer that are especially fond of acorns.

After the wash is hung, Mom and Ruth head for the garden to dig the sweet potatoes and start moving the houseplants indoors. A killing frost last week finished the garden for this year.

The baby tears, spider plants and other houseplants did very well in their partly shaded corner. They are split, trimmed, potted and moved indoors.

In the shoe shop, we are fairly busy getting ready for our annual "Fall Boot Sale" later this week. Emanuel says he hopes to go hunting in the late afternoon, but then daughter Lena stops in to ask if he can help brother-in-law Christ bale hay at about 5 p.m. That takes care of his time.

Daughter Ada comes by with her three little boys on the pony cart, and Grandpa (that's me) is appointed babysitter for a spell while Ruth goes with her to visit Florence Young, an 82-year-old widow who lives back along the mountain. Little 5-week old Emanuel is soon handed over to Mom. Moms are so much better at keeping little ones contented.

"We're preparing for our fall boot sale..."

Supper consists of sweet potatoes and corn fritters, along with apple cider and pineapple buns. It is taken on the run between customers, since we have our shop open until 8 on Monday evenings.

After supper, daughter Anna Mary comes by on a pony cart with her four youngest ones. She is on her way to the market and wants to check if Mom needs anything.

At 9 p.m. Ruth is in bed, Emanuel is in the bath, Mom is crocheting and yours truly is trying to wrap up another busy day.

One more chore remains—marking report cards for the dozen vocational class pupils who assemble at our house for a weekly 3-hour-long class each Tuesday morning. (After matching wits with a dozen lively pupils, I sometimes wonder if I'm teaching or being taught!)

We'll sign off with good night.

Bonnie Nance

BUCKLE UP! Pony cart has no seat belts, but there are plenty of straps and buckles for grandkids to fasten before taking to the road.

CHAPTER FIVE

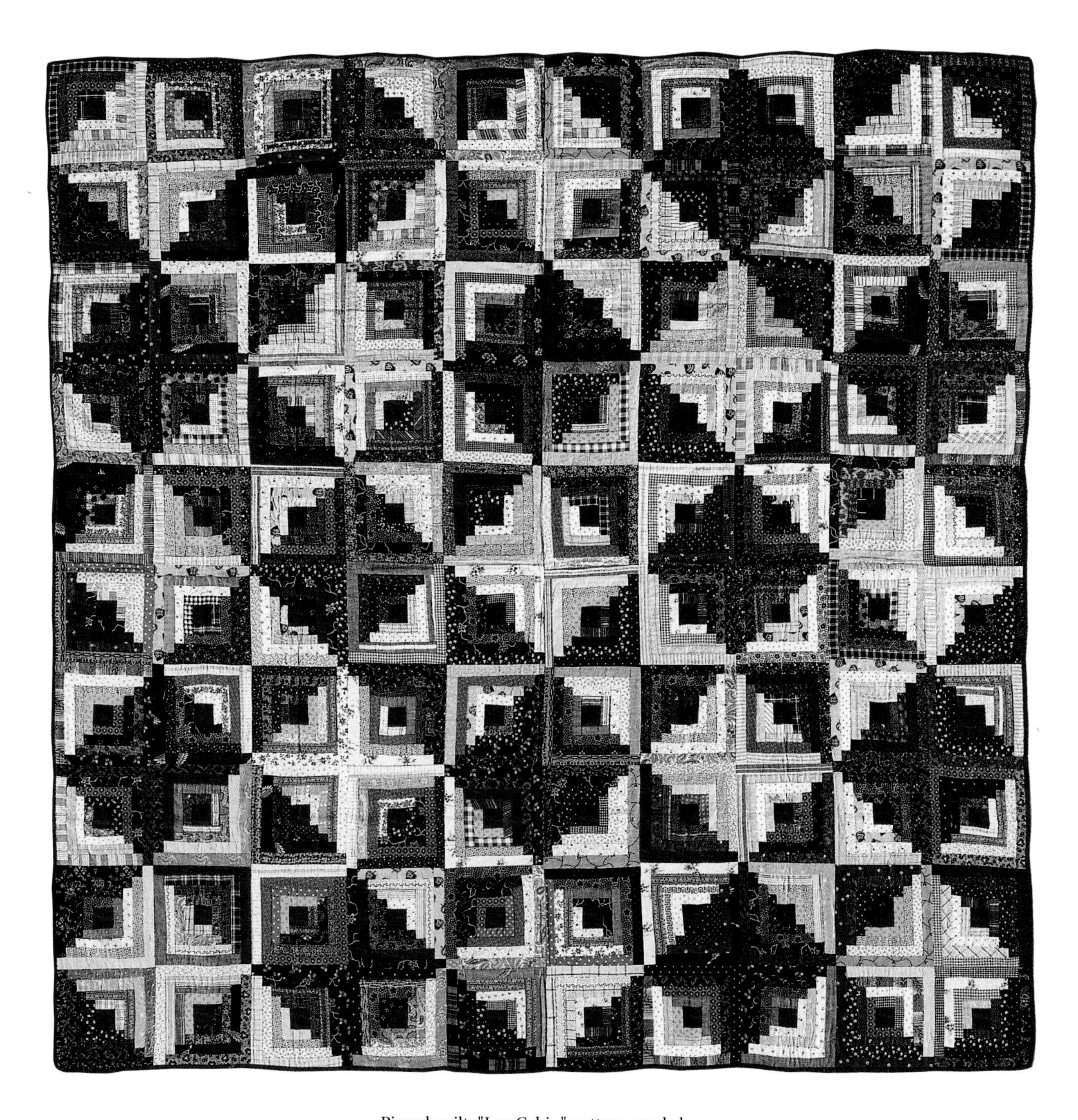

Pieced quilt, "Log Cabin" pattern, made by
Sally Echter Bicker, Lancaster County, c. 1897-1898.

Betty Smithart

A QUIET TIME. Doing without many of the modern conveniences some people take for granted means long hours of hard work, but the Amish still find time for reflection and meditation.

Silo-Filling Crew Will Need a Big Meal

◆ PROFILE ◆

Reuben and Linda Miller farm 95 acres, growing oats, corn and hay. They have some beef cows and calves, 30 sows, chickens and one milk cow. Their children are Joanna, 8, Jason, 6, David, 5, Miriam, 4, Timothy, 2, and Martha, 1. Linda kept this diary.

Bill Hentosh

SCENIC SHOCKS of corn will soon be removed from fields and silos filled with winter feed.

Up at 5 to a pretty, moonlit and windy morning. I started a fire in the kitchen range, and Reuben carried water to do the weekly laundry. (We have running cold water, but haven't set up our wood-burning water heater yet, so we heat it on the cookstove.)

The children were all sleeping yet as we went out to do the chores. I milked the cow, then came in to fix breakfast while Reuben fed the sows and pigs.

I got Joanna up at 6 to do some homework. Jason got up at 6:30 and set the table for breakfast, which consisted of sausage, toast and eggs, homemade grape-nuts and cornflakes.

For their lunches, Joanna fixed sandwiches, and Jason put in some yogurt (a treat) and brownies. Often they like to take lemonade in their thermoses, but today they just put in water.

"There's plenty to keep a crew of 9 or 10 men busy..."

In the *Budget* last night, we read that a little friend, Rosanna Yoder, got hurt and would be in bed for 3 weeks, so Joanna got a card ready for her before going to school.

David and Miriam did the breakfast dishes while I started the laundry. Meantime, Dad and brother Jacob helped Reuben open the cornfield to binder corn.

They use three horses in the binder, cutting one row at a time. Because of weather conditions this year, the corn isn't doing nearly as well as usual.

Tomorrow several neighbors will help fill the silo. That means a big meal, which is enjoyable, too. Mom came up this afternoon and helped me butcher three roosters and bake the pies. The rest of the menu will be dressing, gravy, vegetables, salad, applesauce and fruit with Jell-O.

This afternoon Rube called for help to get another horse in from the pasture. After changing horses, the men kept on bindering till dark, but weren't quite done. There'll be plenty to keep a crew of 9 or 10 men busy tomorrow.

Before starting chores, I sent sandwiches out to the field. Later, the children and I sat down to our supper of chili soup and peaches. Reuben didn't come in till past 9:30, tired from a full and busy day.

Thank you, Lord, for the blessings of another day!

WE HAVE two horses. "Bob" is a big black gelding, safe and reliable. "Max" is big and brown but not so trustworthy, as he did back me in a ditch and laid the buggy on the side a year ago because someone had an empty 10-gallon garbage can lying on the road, rolling with the wind.

We also have a little white Eskimo dog, 3 years old. He likes attention and is jealous of the grandchildren when they are here.

Recently granddaughters Lisa, 4, and JoAnn, 2, stayed with me while their mother, daughter-in-law Mary, had a dentist's appointment.

The girls and I had toasted cheese sandwiches and chili soup for lunch, and in the afternoon we sat outside on the south steps in the sun. I don't know how many trips the little girls made running around the house!

It reminded Lisa of summer, when we have ice cream in a glass with pop added. So we each had a little of that to taste.

While I was sitting outside with a girl on each side, our little dog would come and slip his nose beneath my arm and try to get just a little closer to me than the girls! *—Miriam Bontranger, Wolcotville, Indiana*

Baby Makes Seven for This Delaware Pair

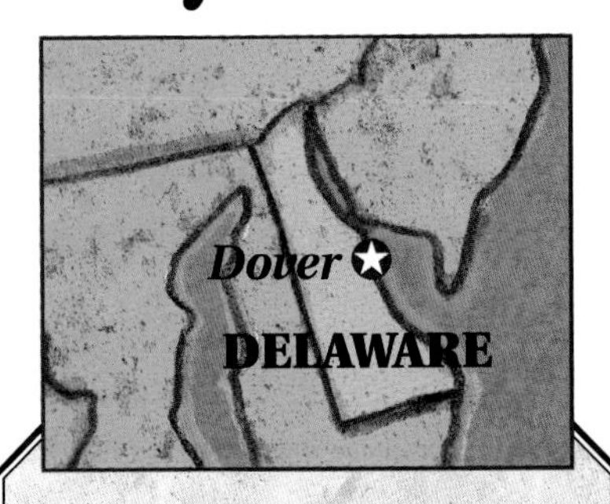

◆ PROFILE ◆

Alvin Hershberger and his wife, Lydia, live on a 3-1/2-acre farm in Kent County near Dover. They have seven children: Wilma, 11, Menno, 9, Esther, 8, Adlai, 7, Alma, 5, Willis, 4, and Alvin Jr., 8 weeks. Alvin works at the Swartzentruber Sawmill & Pallet shop, which makes between 400 and 500 pallets a day. Lydia kept this diary.

RISE AND SHINE. Monday mornings are especially active in the Hershberger home (left) as Lydia cleans up from weekend and gets the children ready for short walk to school (right).

WASH LINE gets a workout from this active family—Lydia and daughter did 20 loads in 2 days!

We got up at 6:30, an hour later than usual. A beautiful day lay before our eyes—the temperature was 48°.

Mondays are usually very busy days for us as we clean up from the weekend. We do baking on Fridays, and on Saturdays Alvin sets up a bake stand. But this past week we didn't bake so I could start some canning. Have more canning for this week.

Alvin and daughter Esther did morning chores, feeding our four horses and two dogs. While I made breakfast, daughter Wilma packed Alvin's lunch, and the boys set the table. We had eggs, toast and cereal.

Alvin left for work at 7 a.m. with "Bud" hitched to the wagon so he could bring home mulch and some corner posts to make a new fence. He has about 3 miles to travel.

The children packed their lunches and washed breakfast dishes. Daughter Wilma and I did six loads of wash and were glad we didn't have more as we did 14 loads on Saturday. Then I braided Esther's and Alma's hair and ironed school clothes before they left for school at 8:45. They only have a little ways up to the road to go.

By then, baby was hungry, so I sat down and fed him, which always takes lots of my time during the day. But we enjoy him very much.

Later, Alvin's niece Barbara Gallaway and son Stephen came. We did her applesauce and canned our tomato juice, and then I watched Stephen while Barbara did some errands in the afternoon.

> *"It was 10 p.m. when the baby finally settled down..."*

When the schoolchildren came home, they changed their clothes in 5 minutes, like usual. Daughter Wilma then went to pick peppers at our neighbor's.

The other girls helped me in the house while the boys did evening chores. Menno came home from school with a bad headache, so he laid down for a nap.

When Alvin came home from work, he put new shoes on Bud. Son Willis, 4, watched him for a while and then said, "Dad, if you get tired, I could take a turn."

For supper we had macaroni and cheese, chicken giblets and fresh applesauce. The children then washed dinner dishes. Baby was fussy, so I took him for a while. Alvin said they made 400 pallets at work today.

After supper, Alvin and Menno mowed some of the lawn and started unloading the mulch Alvin brought home from work. Esther did her arithmetic she didn't get done in school, and the other children colored in their coloring books. Later Alvin looked at his favorite "wish book", the Bass Pro Shop catalog.

Everyone else went to bed at 9:30, but I was up with baby until 10, when he finally settled down.

This sure was a full day for all of us! Let's not forget to be thankful for everything.

Robin Coventry

AS I DO my evening chores, there seems to be a mystery in the family atmosphere, which I mistrust for some surprise they have planned.

The usual suppertime signal hasn't been given, and—aha!—here arrive our three married children, one family at a time, until they and our 17 grandchildren are all present. The kitchen table is lengthened, chairs and benches arranged, and soon homemade pizza, salad, and dessert of ice cream, cookies and cake are put out as well.

Yes, they want to celebrate our two birthdays—my 67th and wife Sarah's 66th. The delicious meal finished and the dishes being washed, the best part of the evening comes—the singing of hymns. Oh, the sweet music filling our house as voices blend together, grandparents with children and grandchildren.

As the singing ends and our guests begin to leave for their homes, we think over our day and can say that it has been a nice and worthwhile one from 5:30 a.m. to 11 p.m. May God be praised.

—Levi Hershberger, Guys Mills, Pennsylvania

Former Farmers Miss Cows, Now Help with Son's Hogs

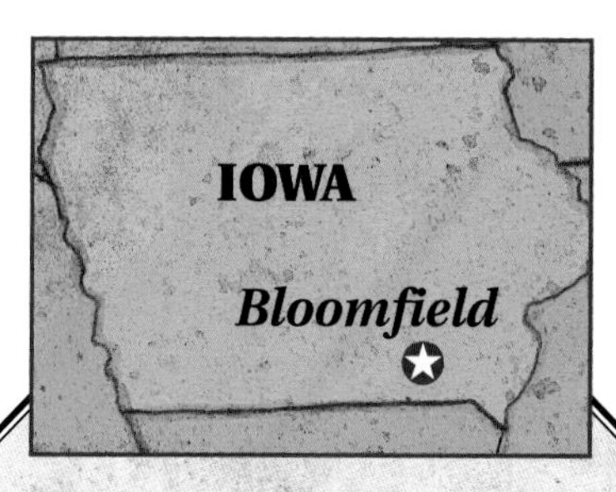

◆ PROFILE ◆

Jake and Mattie Schwartz live on a 73-acre farm outside Bloomfield. Jake no longer farms because of his arthritis. Mattie does quilting in her spare time. The Schwartzes' two children, adopted as infants, are now married. Mattie kept this diary.

Today was a very nice fall day full of "bright blue weather". This surely describes all the days of October so far.

I used to like this month best of all because I have a birthday. But anymore, birthdays aren't so important when you're a senior...and they come earlier than they used to, seems like. Still, I would not want to turn back.

Ben Coblentz

REAL HORSEPOWER. Working dogs and big Belgians are a common sight on most Amish farms.

We started our day earlier than usual as we had overnight company and they planned to leave for their home at Ludington, Michigan by 6 a.m.

I got up at 5 (the alarm went off half an hour earlier because I need time to wake up) to prepare a breakfast of pancakes, tomato gravy and cold cereal.

Jake and I are not farming anymore since selling most of our tools a year ago. It is rather hard not to see cows on pasture and calves romping about, which we were used to.

Due to Jake's arthritic condition in one ankle, uneven or muddy ground underfoot did not agree with his walking. Now he has a job at the sawmill 1/4 mile away, where he can sit on a stool and operate the band saw making pallet lumber. We rented our farmland of 73 acres this year.

I am doing what I like in my spare time, and that's what a lot of grandmas are doing—quilting. Today I got in about 25 yards.

Our son, his wife and our 1-year-old grandson (our first and only grandchild) live behind our home in a trailer and raise hogs. Today our son had some help to work on his gestation building, 

which we call a frolic. Jake served as a gopher (go-for) with horse and buggy to keep the crew busy, as the sawmill where he works is doing repair work and remodeling at present.

At 1 I stirred up a double batch of cinnamon rolls for the mid-afternoon break out there. But at the time to be served, the cement truck came, so the men were delayed an hour in their snack.

We also served two pots of hot tea, which feels pretty good when the weather is a bit chilly, although I suppose they were warmed up by then from doing cement work. It took a large pan of rolls so there'd be two each for six men.

I watched our grandson while his mother mowed the lawn. We've been kept real busy all summer due to ample rainfall. Some fall gardens have been doing pretty good and tasting likewise. Lettuce is appearing on tables in church.

"GOPHER" BUGGY. Jake Schwartz spent the day as a "go-for", running errands in his buggy.

Our flock of 28 hens keeps us and our 3 children in eggs mostly, however today they only laid six, so I guess they are thinking of a rest, too.

We have two workhorses, "Jim" and "Dan". They're real fat from doing only small jobs hauling wood, manure and grinding for the hogs. But at times they'll work for the neighbors.

We each have one buggy horse besides, and that names our animals except 10 cats and a dog named "Echo", who is about 14 years old. He is a good watcher and chaser.

By 9 p.m. Jake was taking his prebedtime nap on the davenport. I was tired, too, with not much to show for it. But then, what can you expect when October 13 rolls around and makes me 62 years old?

Whole Family Helps Prepare for Chicks

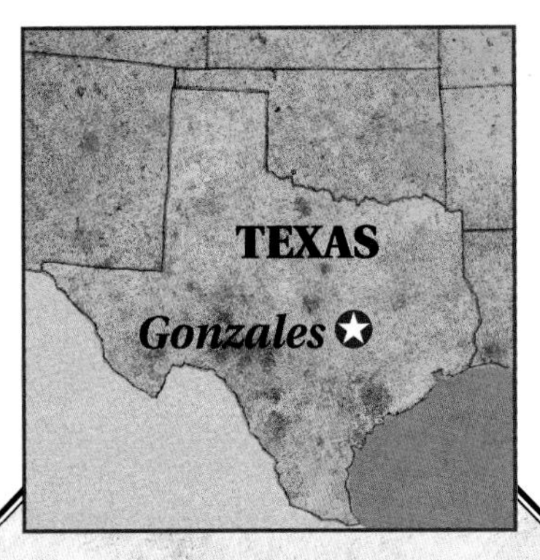

◆ PROFILE ◆

Joe and Katy Ann Hershberger manage a 190-acre ranch near Gonzales, where they make hay, raise 50 mama cows and feed 100,000 broilers every 8-9 weeks. In addition, Joe operates a buggy repair shop. The Hershbergers have six children still at home: Leon, 17, Marc, 16, Sara, 13, Sharon, 9, Joseph Jr., 6, and Amanda, 3. Katy Ann kept this diary.

The alarm went off at 6 a.m. I got up and got everyone awake, then went outside to milk our Jersey cow and feed the rabbits. It was just becoming daylight; the 62° temperature felt almost chilly after a summer of steady 90° weather.

Mist was rising over the fields as the sun came up. Early morning sounds could be heard real clear from neighboring ranches. October mornings are to be relished!

While I was milking, Joe got the children organized. They picked up around the house and took out the garbage, and Sara made a German chocolate cake for tonight's supper.

Breakfast was scrambled eggs in flour tortillas with sour cream and picante sauce, plus fresh pond catfish fried in cornmeal.

There was no school today, and that was real handy because we were getting ready for 100,000 baby chicks to be delivered tomorrow morning.

We started raising baby chicks to boilers 8 years ago today. After lots of upgrading as we went along, work is easier now, with more automatic equipment.

Joe also has a buggy shop called "Gonzales Buggy Works". He works in it whenever ranch work allows some time. Right now he's building a buggy for son Leon. Last week he delivered an open buggy and a breaking cart. There are two wheels waiting for repairs this week yet.

A BIG THIRST. Amanda, 3, takes a break from helping her brothers and sisters in the poultry house.

Joe left for the chicken houses while we cleaned up the kitchen. We joined him at 9:30. Sara, Sharon, Joseph and I put feed into the feed line pans, then filled feed lids, which we put down for baby chicks. These need to be replenished each day until chicks are comfortable with the feed line pans.

Amanda, 3, quickly tired of the activity...nobody would let her help! Joe needed to go to Gonzales for supplies, so we persuaded him to take Amanda to town with him. When they returned,

Bill Hentosh

PERFECT PORCH. Screened porch behind Hershbergers' home is a great place to relax after finishing the gardening, cattle and poultry chores.

PLENTIFUL PEEPERS. Hatchery worker unloads chicks in just-cleaned poultry house. Family raises 100,000 birds every 8-9 weeks.

lunch was sandwiches and leftovers.

Afterward, Joe put insecticide around the chicken houses to keep fire ants out. Once feed is put down, the ants will form up in long lines and carry the feed back to their hills!

The children and I went to check on the garden. We have not had much rain and have been watering the fall crops every 3 days.

Corn is in tassel now, so we hope to be eating fresh corn on the cob in about 3 weeks. The tomatoes are coming on real well. Last week I planted cabbage, cauliflower, broccoli and brussels sprouts, and they all needed water.

"Fire ants steal food from poultry house..."

This evening we sat on the porch steps and watched the sun go down while supper was cooking. Sara had trouble milking the cow (it kicked over the bucket and wouldn't stand still), so she took over mashing the potatoes while I finished milking.

For supper we had roast beef, mashed potatoes and gravy, homegrown peas and German chocolate cake.

We were all in bed by 9:30 p.m., with the sounds of a gentle southern breeze and the crickets chirping to sing us to sleep.

Harness Making and Sewing Fill Retired Farmers' Days

◆ PROFILE ◆

After farming near Millersburg, Ohio for 35 years, Myron and Frieda Mast turned the operation over to son Norman and his wife, Lorene. Now Myron runs a harness shop, making harnesses in all sizes. The Masts have eight sons and three daughters, ages 17 to 34. Frieda kept this diary.

We started out this day bright and early as usual. Myron lit his lantern and headed for his harness shop at 5 a.m. He always was an early riser.

I helped the boys with their lunches, then wrote the *Budget* letter, did desk work and worked on my quilts until 7. By then the rest of the family was ready for breakfast, which is usually a simple one of cold cereal, cookies and coffee.

Daughter Melva did the laundry for us today, and also for her sister Wilma, who has a 5-week-old baby girl named

"Myron came in with six buckets of tomatoes..."

Melissa. Melva should know how laundry goes, as she was also doing it for her brother, who has a 7-week-old baby named Mervin. For several weeks she washed for all three families twice a week.

Daughter Laura, age 23, helps her dad in the harness shop, making harnesses in all sizes. Today they will send out two UPS shipments.

This morning I started on a pieced Schoolhouse quilt. I am also working on some Christmas design orders.

Dinnertime snuck up on me before I realized it, so I quick fixed some grilled ham and cheese sandwiches plus cake and chocolate milk and coffee. We usually have a cooked meal in the evening when all the boys are here.

We have eight boys and three girls, six married. Our married ones all live in walking distance. We have 14 grandchildren, seven boys and seven girls.

After lunch, I told Dad I'd like to have some more tomatoes in before Jack Frost gets them, so he said he'd fetch them. He came back with six big buckets full of tomatoes, so that meant some work yet.

Later I went to help daughter Wilma put one of my Star wall hangings in a

David Miller

Amos Graber

A STITCH IN TIME. Following 35 years of farming, Myron Mast now keeps busy sewing harnesses with help from daughter Laura. Diarist Frieda does sewing on a battery-powered machine.

frame. When I came home this evening, I was surprised to see some delicious-looking "Bob Andy" pie ready for supper.

Melva also had mashed potatoes, gravy, noodles, ham and applesauce ready.

After the supper dishes were all done, I did a few quick stitches on my battery-powered Bernina sewing machine and ironed our capes and aprons which were worn for Communion services yesterday.

We also had short Communion last night for widow Susie Swartzentruber, who is 92 years old and not able to come to church anymore. She has been a widow for 65 years.

One more job waited—Dad needed a haircut. My "barbershop" is open almost all times.

Then the clock said 10 p.m., and it was bedtime.

Anna Wickey

WELL-STOCKED. Frieda's shelves are already filled with jars of fruits and vegetables, but six big buckets full of tomatoes meant more work canning during an already busy diary day.

❖ Are Amish Communities Growing or Declining? ❖

DESPITE an increase in the number of Amish who leave the order each year—some estimate that one out of every five leaves today—most Amish communities are seeing steady growth. In fact, one study shows the Old Order Amish represents one of the fastest-growing religions in the U.S.

The reason for this growth is the large families the Amish continue to have. Today, Amish parents still average between seven and eight children. Many farm families will have 10 or more children.

Since farming is still by far the No. 1 occupation of the Amish, large families are needed because—without electricity or mechanization—an Amish farm is extremely labor-intensive. When cows are still milked by hand and hay still gathered with a team of horses and multiple hayforks, it takes many hands to get the job done.

What's more, divorce and separation are virtually unheard of in Amish communities. Amish children are nurtured and loved as warmly if not more warmly than most children; and they grow up knowing that they're important, their help is needed and that in turn their every need from cradle to grave will be provided by their family, their community and their church.

The cohesiveness of an Amish family is likely unmatched by any other segment of our society.

Robin Coventry

Amish Softball's a Hit!

An "English" photographer came across this lively game at a one-room schoolhouse.

By Pat Crowe, Wilmington, Delaware

IT COULD EASILY have been a scene from the days of Abner Doubleday.

I was driving along a scenic two-lane country road in Lancaster County, Pennsylvania when I passed a one-room schoolhouse where Amish and Mennonite children were playing softball during their noon recess.

I pulled to a stop and was immediately impressed by the spirit and intensity of the game. They played as though it was a major league play-off event. Some assumed the batting stance of Wade Boggs, others fielded like Ozzie Smith—but then I remembered that none of them had television to study those players.

While now and then there were peals of laughter, there were constant shouts of "Strike him out!" They were surrounded by cornfields, but these children—ranging in age from 9 to 13—were as serious about this noon-hour game as their community is about its way of life.

Bright blue shirts, long green dresses and purple bonnets bounced as they ran and slid and swung for all they were worth.

"What's the score?" someone shouted. "It's 25 to 14, but we'll score lots of runs this inning," yelled back a young girl from the team with 15 players.

What impressed me most was the teacher, who not only played with the children but could hit the ball a country mile and field with ease. She showed as much or more zest for this game as her young students.

As I drove away, I thought how fortunate these children are. If they are taught in class with the same enthusiasm and intensity their teacher displayed on the softball field, then the students in this little one-room school get an extraordinary education.

Wisconsinites Well-Known for Belgians

◆ PROFILE ◆

Emanuel and Edna Helmuth grow hay and corn and raise registered Belgian horses in partnership with son Wilbur on their small farm near Evansville. In addition, "Em" and son Daniel, 19, work as carpenters, and Edna has a quilt business. Son David recently completed a historic cross-country trek driving Country's Reminisce Hitch. Edna kept this diary.

BEAUTIFUL BELGIANS raised on Helmuths' farm are a pleasing sight for folks passing by.

Got up at 5:45. The men went out to feed the sows and pigs while I fixed two lunches and made our breakfast of pancakes, syrup, eggs and oatmeal, also spearmint tea that we grow in the garden.

At 6:45 comes Daniel's driver; they go to Evansville today to put siding on a house. At 7 comes Emanuel's driver; they are working at Cross Plains putting up a horse barn.

I do the dishes and have the day to myself, like always. You may think I'd have long days, but it seems they are never long enough! Today I did the laundry first. With such a beautiful morning, I decided to hang the clothes all outside. Then I cleaned and brushed the men's Sunday suits that were worn to church yesterday.

"I made 22 pints of grape jelly today..."

Next I went out and gathered grapes, picked off the stems and cooked the grapes for jelly. At noon the mailman left a *Farm & Ranch Living* magazine in the box, so I glanced through it while having a sandwich and some chocolate milk.

This afternoon a quilt customer came to pick up a crib quilt that she had ordered. The grapes were still cooking, so I went and got in the clothes that were dry and ironed a couple pieces yet, then went back to my jelly. I ended up making 22 pints! By then it was time to start supper.

Daniel came home at mid-afternoon, as they finished the job in Evansville. Starting tomorrow, they'll have a remodeling job in Brodhead for the rest of the week, then to Janesville to start another new house. So Daniel cleaned out hog pens this afternoon.

Em didn't get home till 7:15, so finally at 7:30 we were ready to eat supper. We had chicken, mashed potatoes and gravy, corn, applesauce, and ice cream and cake.

Tonight David called to say the Hitch was at Peoria, Illinois. By 8:20 we were all ready for bed after a full day.

SIZABLE STRUCTURE. Helmuths' barn is appropriately large for housing the horses they raise. Silos in back store feed. Right: Edna's latest quilt is displayed.

IN THE afternoon, Verna Weaver and her daughter Jolene, and Louella Yoder and her son and daughter came over to help make doughnuts. I usually make 10 dozen at a time, along with four loaves of bread.

Verna and I had the first batch of doughnuts rising in the warm oven when Louella came. Verna was washing dishes, and I was kneading my bread when I decided I'd better stop and check on my doughnut dough.

Horrors! I had mixed it in a bowl that was too small, and there was dough all over the oven—a stringy and gooey mess!

We decided we might as well laugh about it. Later, the men and schoolchildren all had fresh doughnuts when they came home. *—Ruth Raber, Millersburg, Ohio*

◆ PROFILE ◆

Orie and Katie Miller grow corn, oats, wheat, hay and soybeans and raise beef cows and hogs on their 57-acre farm near Mount Vernon. Of their six children, one son, David, 25, still lives at home. Orie kept this diary.

Heating Up the Wash Water Is This Day's First Chore

Up at 5, my usual time. I went out and checked a sow in the farrowing house; she was okay, so I came in, washed up and helped Katie get breakfast of fried eggs, toast, orange juice, cereal and coffee. After devotions, David left for work.

Since we don't milk cows, the chores usually wait till daylight. Meantime, I got some mail ready. I write the local news for three different newspapers, *The Budget*, *The Botshaft* and *Gemeinda Register*. Then I went out to the wash house and started a fire in the old feed cooker to heat rainwater.

Katie likes rainwater to wash so she can use homemade soap, which she makes with animal fats and lye. It works best in soft water.

Katie did the dishes, cleaned up the house and got the wash ready. When the water was hot, I helped her get the wash out and started the motor.

After I was done choring, I walked 

up the road to the freezer house where we and eight other families have our freezers. Using the phone there, I made an appointment with a local man who has a press to get some cider made later on this week.

Back home, I finished putting the box on the wagon to husk corn on, then took a hub off our gravity wagon to take to our welder, who's making steel wheels for it. Next I got the horses in and fed them.

By that time, dinner was ready. We had mostly leftovers from last night—macaroni, hot dogs, sliced tomatoes, applesauce, pumpkin, custard and Oreo cookie pudding.

After a short nap, I hitched our big Belgians, "Pearl" and "Nell", to the wagon and went for the cornfield, where I husked one round and opened up the field.

"Katie uses rainwater for the washing..."

Katie finished the wash and worked in the garden, getting in some late vegetables, cleaning flower beds and spading some.

It was about 3:30 when I got home, unloaded the corn and put the wagon away. Then I hitched "Lady", our road horse, to the two-wheeled cart and took that hub down to the welder man. When I got back, I had to mix up a batch of chicken feed. David was home and helped chore.

For supper we had potluck potatoes, wieners, sliced tomatoes and some leftover custard and pudding from dinner.

By 9:15 we were all tired and ready for bed.

Don Shenk

CHAPTER SIX

Pieced quilt, "Pine Tree" pattern, made by
Sarah Shenk of East Petersburg area,
Lancaster County, c. 1875-1895.

R.K. OLEJNICZAK

DIPPING A LINE. Once the chores are done, many Amish enjoy fishing or hunting. Such "sports" are relaxing but also help to fill up pantry shelves and freezer lockers with fish and meats.

'Mom', 'Dad' Double Up On Diary-Keeping Duties

◆ **PROFILE** ◆

Jerry and Susie Miller milk 12 to 18 cows by hand and farrow 16 sows on their farm located near Middlebury. Jerry also works for a fertilizer dealer, helping to analyze soil samples. The Miller children are Joas, 16, Elsie, 15, Clarence, 13, Dorcas, 11, and Miriam, 10. Jerry and Susie each wrote their own separate diary. (Jerry's comes first, followed by Susie's.)

At 4:20 a.m. I hear something far, far away, coming closer. Is it the ready-mix truck backing up? Oh, it's the beeping of the alarm clock!

Swinging out of bed, I dress and light the two gas and one kerosene lanterns. Susie arises a few minutes later and hustles around doing early morning tasks, awakening the children and rekindling the wood fire in the kitchen range to make sure there's hot water to take out and wash the cows' udders.

Leaving the house about 15 minutes later, I glance at the old faithful thermometer—46°. It is a beautiful starlit morning with a slight breeze out of the south. Should be a good day to cultipack that newly-sowed wheat field!

Coming out to the barn, I see the cows had come up already and a few are lying down in the tramp shed. Oh, my! Yesterday was Sunday, and we usually don't bed them on the Lord's day. Now a few of those cows are quite dirty, which I know won't make Mom happy when she comes out to milk. Sorry!

"Heah, Fido, heah," I call. Hearing our border collie's loud woof, the cows that had relaxed quickly get up. I proceed over to the cow stable.

I measure out feed and let the first nine cows into their stanchions. I hear Susie getting the strainers on the milk cans, and the children dropping by, one by one, sleepy-eyed.

Zing, Zing. Next I hear the rapid streams of milk against the pails as everybody gets into the act of milking. Presently, the call comes, "What are we going to do today, Dad?"

"That field we sowed wheat in Saturday needs to be cultipacked and stones picked up," I say. "Also, today, that backhoe digger is coming to replace that old faulty water line buried under the driveway."

Coming back to the cow stable, the two youngest girls, Dorcas and Miriam, are done with their cows. We let out those which are milked and let the last five cows in. Now our 12 calves are pleading to have their breakfast, so the girls feed them with their milk bottles, while the rest of us finish milking.

About 6, Mom goes in to start breakfast. Elsie washes milk utensils, Joas feeds hay to the cows and Clarence runs an errand to one of the neighbors. I jog down to the neighbor telephone (put there for Amish use) to make a phone call. I want to get a taxi driver to take me to tomorrow's special education meeting about 30 miles away.

Back home, it's time for us to go for breakfast. Joas has the 10 horses in their stalls and fed. And here comes Clarence riding full speed. Watch out! Not so fast! We kick off our boots and go wash up.

"Today the backhoe is coming to replace a bad water line..."

Breakfast is Pennsylvania-style eggs and crackers. "No bread," Mom says, so we'll have crackers.

While eating, there is a knock on the door, and a neighbor asks if he may use our grinder-mixer to grind feed for his cows. Yes, of course; it would suit best in the afternoon if that backhoe comes this morning as he promised.

By 7:30, we're sitting in the living room, having devotions, which is a vital part of our life.

After devotions, everyone goes about their tasks. Clarence cleans the cow stable before school time, Joas feeds his rabbits and I feed the hogs. Girls quickly wash the morning dishes. Children take off for school.

It's 8:30, and I expect my backhoe man any minute. Joas has hitched "Max" and "Dolly", the draft horses, to the cultipacker, and he says we need a new stone box if we want to gather up stones while packing.

In a few minutes we make a new stone box while I have an ear tuned to hear the backhoe when he shows up.

It's 9 o'clock, and Joas and Elsie are at last ready to go to the field to pack down the earth and small stones, as we will have hay in the field after wheat. Any stone bigger than a softball goes into the stone box and is deposited on a pile at one end of the field.

It's a beautiful, clear and sunny day! Why doesn't this backhoe show up? Oh, well...I'm not always on time, either!

Getting out an old barrel, I cut it in half with a cold chisel to make a new water tank for the calves. Taking it out to the calf pen, I start filling it at the hydrant while setting up a feeder for grain. I chase four yearlings into this pen and shut off my water. 9:30 and the backhoe is still not here.

We can hardly get water up to the house anymore from the pumphouse, so I now go for the phone to see why this man doesn't show up. Glancing out toward the field, I see Joas and Elsie have made a lot of progress. Walking past the garden, I see Susie is clearing it from its summer leftovers.

Calling up my backhoe man, I'm surprised to find him at home at this time of the day. He's also surprised and doesn't know what to say—he has plumb forgotten our arrangement! Yes, he will be here right after lunch.

I come home, empty a little red wagonload of plants Susie has pulled out and fix a few door closers. At 11:30 I 

sharpen the chain saw yet, so we can cut up that old fallen-down elm tree before winter comes. Joas and Elsie come up for dinner, being hungry as bears after picking stones all forenoon.

After a hearty dinner, we relax a few minutes in the living room. At 1:15, I wake up and tell Joas it's time to go. Joas hitches to the cultipacker but, sorry, Elsie has to help Mom.

At 1:30, the backhoe man finally shows up, and Joas can't go to the field for awhile. After all, we don't have a backhoe in here every day!

Bill Miller is pretty good at it, and the backhoe quickly digs out the old pipeline. In 4 hours, we have replaced 45 feet of waterline, 5 feet below the surface. Around 3:30, we have an audience when the scholars come home.

The $171 worth of new water pipe is pumping our supply tanks full, and the backhoe man leaves around 5:30. Mom is happy, and Dad is relieved.

Mom and the children start milking. Joas is done with his job, stones all in neat piles along the end of the field. I go milking and in for supper around 7.

We are done with supper at 8. Mom and Elsie go on a walk, and here I sit after having evening devotions and sending the children to bed.

Now it's 9:40, so good night.

Except the Lord build the house, they labor in vain that build it.

(Susie's diary)

R-r-ring! The alarm went off, and Jerry was out of bed at once. I followed soon after, got dressed and started the fire in my beloved "Pioneer Maid" kitchen range. It feels good to the family to awaken to a cozy kitchen.

At 4:45 I waked each of the children, starting with the oldest, telling them, "Time to go milk!" I waited briefly till I heard everyone's sleepy, faint "yes" before going to the cow barn.

Why Don't They Want Their Pictures Taken?

TOURISTS in Amish communities soon learn that it is neither courteous nor respectful to ask adult Amish to pose for photographs. Nor do they want you to take "unposed" pictures of them. They don't want you to take pictures of them, period!

They usually don't mind you taking pictures of their children, but once they become "of age"—that is, in their late teens when they become a member of the adult community—they are opposed to having photographs taken.

Their opposition is based on the Second Commandment: *"Thou shalt not make unto thee any graven image, or any likeness of anything that is in heaven above, or that is in the earth beneath, or that is in the water under the earth."* (Exodus 20:4)

Less technically, it's because the Amish are taught to avoid any form of vanity, pride or conceit. Posing for pictures and then displaying those photos of themselves would be contrary to this belief.

After milking "my" cows, I came back in and got breakfast started while Dorcas fixed three school lunches and Miriam set the table. Along with getting breakfast, I cooked a large batch of cherry pie filling to be made into pies later in the day.

Breakfast done, Elsie washed the dishes while the other two girls got ready for school. I started bread dough. While that was rising, I went out to the garden and started cleaning it off. The garden produce is past now, so we'll pull up all the old tomato, pepper, bean and flower plants and throw them out to the hogs.

Before pulling up the flower plants, I got a small bowl from the house and gathered into it flower seeds to dry and store, then sow in next year's garden. One of my neighbor ladies happened to stop by at this time, so I shared some of my seeds with her.

By then it was 10:30 and time to put bread in the oven, plus get dinner. I got the meal started cooking, then baked my cherry pies while the potatoes cooked and the Poor Man's Steak simmered.

While decorating my top pie crust, I absentmindedly marked it with "A" for apple instead of "C" for cherry, so we had that "mistake" for dessert at dinner.

As we were eating, I read aloud to the family our letter from Reiman Publications that came in the mail today. While doing that, I burned the last pie in the oven! (Clarence loves burned food, so that won't be a problem.)

After the noon rest, Elsie and I both worked in the garden. With the beautiful weather, it was truly wonderful being out under the clear blue sky and warm sun. All around the house, the tall maples were starting to dress in their golden fall colors. In a setting as that, one is happy just to be alive!

In between the garden work, I found time to skip in the house while it was quiet to write my circle letter. Meanwhile, the children came home from school, and, after snacking on fresh bread and black cherry pie, the two girls washed dinner and lunch bucket dishes.

After that, they filled the wood box and fed the chickens. In between, everybody found time to watch the backhoe digger at work out by the barn. Then it was milking time again at 5 p.m.

For supper, I fixed garden oyster soup and sandwiches. Dessert was cherry pie sauce over fresh bread with milk.

After supper, Elsie and I went on our

health walk and stopped by the neighbors' to plan with them to butcher my chickens one day early next week.

All in all, we had a good day, and at bedtime we could say, "Yes, tired but happy!"

PLENTY OF PULL. Susie Miller spent a busy afternoon in her garden pulling up old vegetable and flower plants. Seeds from the flowers will be saved for next year's planting.

Quilter Has Years of 'Diary' Experience

◆ PROFILE ◆

Abe and Edna Miller live on a 140-acre farm near Mt. Hope, Ohio, where they milk 14 cows by hand and grow corn, hay, oats and barley. Edna, who makes quilts and wall hangings for sale, has been a regular diarist for Country and Country EXTRA magazines for several years. Three of the Millers' four children still live at home: Dorothy, 28, Leroy, 23, and Leon, 19.

It is very chilly this morning as I head for the barn. The stars are all shining, and it looks like it could be a beautiful day.

After milking the cows by hand, bottle-feeding the calves and washing the buckets, I head for the house. There isn't a cloud in sight, and the sky is so very clear and blue.

It's wash day, so while the wash tubs fill with water, I sort the wash, and Abe starts the motor. While those first loads of wash are scrubbing, I walk out to our grape arbor and eat a few grapes. When I make jelly, I always leave some to eat later on. On a chilly morning like this, they are cold and oh, so sweet.

Soon I have all the laundry done and hung on the line to dry, flapping in the wind. It has turned out to be such a beautiful day.

Abe cleans the baler and grain drill and puts them in the shed since winter will soon be here. Then he sorts the potatoes for me and puts them in the cellar. I scrub the little potatoes and put them through the salad master before canning them.

GIDDAP, THERE! Miniature sulky is lots of fun for the Millers' grandsons, who take turns riding and pulling.

This afternoon, I can the little pota- 

STITCHED IN TIME. Her customers wait patiently for Edna's colorful quilts and wall hangings.

toes with the pressure cooker. Trying to get supper and watching the pressure sure keeps me hopping.

Our daughter Dorothy comes home from work and helps me with supper. We have mashed potatoes, mixed vegetables, applesauce and squirrel I had put into the oven earlier.

I am not at the least bit hungry for squirrel, but both boys, Leroy and Leon, think the taste is out of this world. They are both hunters, so no wonder!

Later, Dorothy mows the lawn while we others do the milking and other chores.

After I am finished in the barn, I take the wash off the line and hang it over my arm. That fresh smell when I am folding those towels reminds me that soon cold weather will set in and I have to hang all that laundry in the basement.

The trees are turning, and as the sun sets in the west, it brings out all the colors and reminds us of God, their maker.

Really, fall is the most beautiful of the seasons; it brings the changing of leaves and soon those very first snowflakes, and making candy, wrapping presents. But let's not forget what Christmas is really about.

The grandchildren are anxious to get out their sleds! Is it really any wonder why fall is so special to me? I love to sit and quilt and watch the snowflakes fly by.

Now, with our last cooker of potatoes off the fire and waiting for the pressure to go down, we sit around the table and have popcorn and cider before going to bed.

The Background on Those Beautiful Buggy Horses

IF you've seen the movies *Witness* or *Friendly Persuasion*, or have had the opportunity to visit an Amish community, you've likely admired the fine-looking horses pulling those black buggies.

"They look like racehorses," tourists often say, and unknowingly they're usually right. Many Amish buggy horses come from the country's harness-racing tracks.

Because they're not quite good enough to win on the circuit or are too old to race, the horses are purchased by brokers and trucked to Amish communities, where they're sold at auctions.

These horses are usually trotters or pacers, which explains why they move along effortlessly and easily cover 10 miles in an hour.

Because the Amish are so dependent on these horses for transportation, they take very good care of them. In many cases, the buggy horse is almost part of the family.

R.K Olejniczak

Independence

IOWA

Circle Letter Brings News From Family and Friends

◆ PROFILE ◆

Jerry and Emma Stutzman have worked their 136-acre farm in Buchanan County since 1959, the second year they were married. Besides harvesting corn, which they husk by hand, they grow beans, oats and hay and milk 13 Holsteins. Of their 13 children, seven are now married. Emma kept this diary.

It was a beautiful October day—windy from the north, temperature at 45° this morning. No frost damage yet.

We were up at 5:15 as milkman comes at 6. Went at our daily chores. Only milk 8 cows now—some are dry—so the girls got the wash water heated and fixed lunch for Edwin, 11, who is our last and only scholar.

I made breakfast of bacon and eggs, muskmelon, cereal and cake. Son Jerry ate before the rest and left with hack-buggy and horse "Max" to feed and take care of his 90 sows with piggies, all out in pasture in hog huts.

After breakfast, Edwin and neighbor boy Freeman Yoder trudged their 1-1/2 mile walk to school. Susie and Barbara did the washing, using two wash machines rigged up with one motor to save time. I butchered our last three fat fryers, salted them to put in the ice house. About 1/3 of our ice is left.

Daughter Emma cleaned Sunday clothes and then picked grapes. I did odd jobs and got some mail ready. Sons Jerry and Freeman went over to son David's to help set up corn shocks, and husband Jerry fixed the hog waterer and repaired barn doors as the weather may get cold soon.

This afternoon the girls did the ironing and mending. The boys came home soon after dinner, so they mowed a round of new hay and brought it in for cows as pasture is getting short. Then Jerry got the binder ready and opened the two bean fields.

We had some extra time yet before chores, so we picked six bushels of Red Delicious apples. We'll pick the rest tomorrow.

Daughter Sadie brought her three little girls over this evening and then went back in the timber to pick up hickory nuts, which are a fair crop this year.

Got my interesting circle letter today. There are nine in the circle, and all have from 13-16 children each. I also worked a bit on a quilt I'm piecing, a Sunrise Star.

By 7:30 the children were all in bed except for Edwin, who is putting together toy fences that we sell at the variety store. Soon it is time for us to hit the hay, too.

Bringing In the Sheaves

WHEAT HARVEST on most modern farms is a fast-paced, automated activity with large combines gobbling up big acres.

That's not so in Lancaster County, Pennsylvania, where the Amish still harvest wheat just as others did years ago. It's a communal event, with a threshing crew moving from farm to farm during the first 2 weeks in July.

First the golden grain is cut and bundled by horse- or mule-drawn binders, then stacked by hand into long lines of symmetrical shocks. Later, when the threshing crew comes, everyone in the family joins in to help.

At first glance these may look like nostalgic old-time photos, but they were taken just recently by photographer Jerry Irwin. Studying them will take you back to an era when farming was less hurried and simpler...and a lot more scenic.

KANSAS

Haven

Heat's Hard on Horses, So They Farm with Tractors

◆ PROFILE ◆

Eli and Katie Miller grow wheat and alfalfa hay and raise beef cattle on their 80-acre century farm near Yoder. Of their eight children (four sons and four daughters), two live at home: Ivan, 18, and Ada Mae, 12. Katie kept this diary.

LOTS OF TREES surrounding the Miller's big old farmhouse help shade the hot Kansas sun.

Our day starts later than usual, at 6:30 a.m., as it is my day off from Yoder Cafe. I've worked there as a baker 4 or 5 days a week for the last 5 years.

I fill the 30-gallon iron kettle with rainwater with a pitcher pump mounted on the kettle from the cistern outside the washhouse. The kettle is enclosed with brick walls inside the washhouse, just the way Grandfather fixed it years ago. We use a propane gas burner (because wood fire with old bricks could be a fire hazard) to heat the water to do my laundry.

Eli does our chores of feeding our two horses, cattle and around 30 chickens, then goes across the road and takes care of the neighbor's horses.

We have a breakfast of fried cornmeal mush, cereal and grape juice before Ada Mae catches the bus for Yoder School, where she is in seventh grade.

After doing dishes, I do our day's laundry with a wringer Maytag washer and Honda motor.

Meantime, Eli harrows ground around the buildings at Enos Keim's place across the road. We farm his wheat ground, and Eli finished sowing wheat there 2 days ago.

"I've canned over 100 quarts of grape juice..."

Enos Keim is 80 years old and had heart bypass surgery in Wichita recently. He is doing real well and hopes to be discharged today.

It is a beautiful day—clear and 58° as I hang the laundry out on the clothesline in a nice breeze. The blue morning glories are still showing their splendor—we have not had a frost yet.

At 10 a.m. Eli and son Ivan go to Yoder for supplies with our horse and spring wagon. Ivan has vacation this week from his job at Sunflower Buggy Shop, which is owned and operated by our son-in-law Sam Yoder and our daughter Kay in Yoder, Kansas, 1-1/2 miles from us.

The shop is well-known; Sam does restorations as well as work on new buggies. He gets orders for working on stage coaches from every state west of here. He has just finished his first new stage coach this week, and Kay is doing the pinstripe painting.

Ivan is the wheelwright and also has been building two spring wagons recently. Sam finished a new cart for a miniature pony last week.

At noon Eli and I have a light lunch of sandwiches, orange Jell-O with fruit cocktail and cake. Following lunch, I get the laundry in, iron and do some mending and lengthening of some of our growing daughter's dresses.

Later I gather Concord grapes in the garden and can 8 quarts of grape juice. To the present, I have canned over 100 quarts total.

While I work in the kitchen, Eli cleans the drill and other machinery.

COZY BEDROOM is brightened by a colorful quilt, some favorite magazines and cute baby doll.

BUSY BUILDING BUGGIES. Son-in-law Sam Yoder's buggy shop is well known in the area. Besides building all types of horse-drawn vehicles (like this hearse), Sam restores and repairs.

We farm with tractors as it is too warm in this region to work horses during the summer—often over 100°. Our wheat harvest is normally in late June and early July, and we plow soon after harvesting.

Our farm of 160 acres was homesteaded by Curtis O'Neal on May 15, 1876. We have the homestead deed signed by President U.S. Grant.

Eli's great-grandfather bought the farm in 1883, having come from Illinois. Later, his son Andy (Eli's grandfather) owned it. Andy died in 1968, and we bought the east 80 with the homestead on it. We moved here soon after our marriage 38 years ago.

Daughter Ada Mae is home from school at 3:15 p.m. and has homework to do. Meanwhile, I reflect on yesterday's news at church while doing a few more chores.

Yesterday we attended church at Jay Bontrager's. We have one bishop, three ministers and one deacon in our church. Our bishop is 80 years old and wants to retire, so the church has voted to ordain one of the ministers as bishop by lot soon.

The members will vote their choice, then the elected ones draw from the lot, so the Lord has a chance to choose the man he wants.

Chores done, we have macaroni and cheese with wieners, green beans, pepper rings and Jell-O for supper.

While Ada Mae does dishes after supper, I pick pears off our trees. These two trees were planted by Great-Grandfather and are loaded with pears. I will can them later. It is also apple-canning time, too.

The temperature made it up to 87° by day's end. Now we have a beautiful full harvest moon. It's 8 p.m. and we're ready to retire for the day, as that alarm clock will go off again at 4:45 tomorrow morning.

Growing Boys Keep Her Busy Sewing and Mending

◆ PROFILE ◆

Floyd and Laureen Miller sell feeder pigs from 100 sows and raise about 90 Leghorn pullets and roosters on their 5-acre farm in Kosciusko County. They have eight children: Karl Dean, 13, Kenneth Allen, 11, Lyle Dale, 10, Melvin Roy, 8, Annabelle, 6, Norma Jean, 5, Calvin, 3, and Maynard, 1-1/2. Floyd works in a trailer factory. Laureen kept this diary.

We got up at 4:45. The temperature was 50°, and the moon and stars were brightly shining. It is so nice and peaceful at that time in the morning.

Floyd fed the sows in the farrowing house. Two sows had pigged during the night, and another was still at it when Floyd went to chore.

I packed his lunch and baked two chocolate cakes from scratch. I am hoping those cakes last till Friday—it takes a lot of eats around here with our growing family.

Floyd had time to read in the New Testament while waiting for his driver to go to Fairmont, a trailer factory in Nappanee where he works.

I filled out the church report for an Amish newsletter called *Die Blatt*, which I do every 2 weeks on Monday after our church. The report consists of where church was, where it's to be next time, visiting ministers, if any, and any other news such as births, wedding announcements, sickness or accidents in the congregation.

By then, it was high time to wake up the four scholars, Karl, seventh grade, Kenneth, sixth grade, Lyle, fourth grade, and Melvin, second grade. They attend Maple Grove school, right across the ditch from us.

Lyle wanted to have chocolate pudding for breakfast when he saw the baking cocoa. We spoon the pudding over bread spread with peanut butter. By the time it was ready to eat, the other four 

children were awake, too. So, we all ate together.

After breakfast, the children did their various chores and by 8 were ready for school.

I had been wanting to make a new bassinet cover for several weeks, and today seemed to be the day I could work it in. Using the old one for a pattern, I cut the material in the forenoon and got over half of it sewed. I got it finished in the afternoon. What a good feeling!

With growing boys, there are always some who need new pants or alterations. Right now, they're all needing new or bigger pants for Sunday. Kenneth and Calvin's are done, and today I cut Karl and Melvin's Sunday pants.

I made two trips to the farrowing house, checking temperature and if more sows were pigging. One gilt was still not sure how to use her nipple waterer, so I tried to show her how. Hope she'll have the hang of it soon!

The boys came home from school for a quick lunch of fried egg sandwiches with sliced tomatoes, green beans and grape cheesecake. They hurried back to school so they wouldn't miss a minute of recess time as they were playing softball.

Last year we had 58 pupils in our school, and it was crowded! So it was decided to put up another school, West Hastings. There are now 28 pupils in our school. If this nice weather stays, Maple Grove's upper four grades get to go visit and play softball at West Hastings on Tuesday, which they really look forward to.

We had popcorn and apples for a snack when the school boys came home. Karl practiced shooting bow and arrow while Kenneth fed the sows in the barn, the sows in the farrowing house, the feeder pigs and our three horses.

Lyle skinned three fryers by himself. Melvin and Norma cleaned up the house. Annabelle helped wash and peel carrots.

Floyd didn't come home from work until 6. He's working ahead so he can take off on Wednesday for a wedding. He started giving shots to the 68 pigs today until we had supper ready.

We made egg rolls for supper, using our own cabbage from the garden. We love egg rolls. (We make the filling by ourselves but buy the skins.) Karl fried them while I rolled them up. We like to dip them in salsa. Also on the menu were new potatoes served with parsley and butter, vegetable dip with fresh broccoli, kohlrabi and carrots.

In the evening we had several people stop in for various things, so Floyd didn't get back out to finish processing pigs.

After some Bible stories, the tired children headed for bed at 9 p.m. Floyd got an order ready for hog vaccines and medication tonight before we went to bed at 10.

WE ALWAYS have a large garden and sell extra produce during summer.

The basement shelves are again nearly full. The list of canned things from the summer is as follows:

37 quarts strawberries, frozen
12 quarts strawberries, canned
8 pints jam, cooked
12 batches freezer jam
34 quarts peas, frozen
8 quarts, 3 pints peas, canned
21 quarts string beans, canned
35 quarts sweet corn, canned
41 quarts sweet corn, frozen
14 quarts bread-and-butter pickles
33 quarts sweet garlic dills
16 quarts, 17 pints sweet pickles
14 quarts blueberries, canned
20 pounds blueberries, frozen
58 quarts tomato juice
28 quarts whole tomatoes
24 pints catsup
16 quarts pizza sauce
16 pints pickle relish
48 quarts peaches, canned
12 quarts peaches, frozen
109 quarts applesauce

—Lydia Stutzman, Clare, Michigan

OUR HIGHWAY, Route 27, is a very busy and dangerous road. It is nothing but curves and hills from Meadville to Titusville, a distance of about 25 miles.

We horse and buggy owners like to have well-equipped safety precautions for night traveling on this road. We use the "slow moving vehicle" emblem and blinking red or amber tail lights. As an extra measure, we use reflecting tape on the back of the buggy so it is outlined. We can't be too safety-conscious on this speedway. *—Levi Hershberger, Guys Mills, Pennsylvania*

Betty Smithhart

Working 'Ropewalk' Helps Keep Him Fit

◆ **PROFILE** ◆

Andrew and Lena Mae Troyer operate the country's only commercial "ropewalk", hand-twisting individual fiber strands into sturdy ropes up to 600 feet long. They moved to Conneautville in 1990 from Apple Creek, Ohio, where the family business started 17 years ago. Now three of Andrew's sisters, Anna, Amanda and Mary, are employees of the growing company. The family also shares an avid interest in bird-watching. The Troyers have five children: Miriam, 15, Ruth, 13, Neva, 9, Adam, 6, and Marcus, 22 months. Andrew kept this diary.

STRONG FAMILY TIES. Once a small sideline, rope making is now a full-time business for Troyer family. Colorful spools of twine (above) will become sturdy ropes sold all across the country.

At 4 a.m. I got up, dressed, emptied the ash pan, shook the grates and added a few more logs to the fire. While emptying the pan outdoors, I noticed that Orion on my left was looking at me, and to my right was the Big Dipper standing on end, pointing at the North Star. The moon was high in the west. It was a very beautiful morning.

Next I got my notes together and wrote my *Budget* letter. I enjoyed a glass of orange juice while working.

6:10 a.m.—I scheduled the day's work, checking the rope orders that were to be filled today, doing various office tasks and feeding our horses.

Meanwhile, Momma and Ruth packed the lunch buckets and got breakfast ready. The buckets each contained a ham with lettuce sandwich, some potato chips, a dish of fruit and a special treat, a Hershey's candy bar.

7 a.m.—After devotions, Bible reading, discussion and a prayer, we had our favorite breakfast of oatmeal blueberry pancakes with old-fashioned oatmeal milk gravy and pure maple syrup. Ummmmmm! I had my coffee in my favorite mug that says "I love my dad", given to me by our dear children.

7:50 a.m.—I had 10 minutes left before shop hours, so I played "stack" with son Marcus, who has Down's syndrome. He loves it when we play and help him look through his books. We love it, too.

8 a.m.—As I got up to go to work, Marcus cried—he didn't want me to leave him. His plea was irresistible, so I just took time off and played some more with him.

8:15 a.m.—Our three school-age children, Ruth, Neva and Adam, left for school. Marcus was satisfied, so I headed for the shop, stopping on the way to feed the bluebirds. How thrilled I am to be able to feed these gems of blue each day!

Miriam did the breakfast dishes while Momma did the laundry. It was a beautiful wash day.

8:50 a.m.—Anna, Amanda and I headed for the ropewalk with tubes of yarn on our cart to make 10 spools (6,000 feet) of 1/2-inch rope. Amanda operated the winder at the far end of the walk, which is 780 feet long, while 

I walked along twisting the strands together.

11:50 a.m.—We were done with the ten spools. I had to walk over 6 miles to fill this order...at least I don't need morning jogs like President Clinton!

12 p.m.—Today's mail contained 22 pieces from 12 different states and Canada. For a change, there were more checks than bills. Our "Nature Friends' Circle Letter", now in its 50th round, also arrived. It has eight members and was started in 1985.

We had sandwiches and popcorn for lunch. Afterward I played with Marcus and then took a 10-minute nap.

1:15 p.m.—Momma put the laundry away, and Miriam did some cleaning. I made that everyone else was doing their jobs (ha!), then harvested this year's crop of gourds, which we will air dry and make into purple martin houses. This year we were thrilled to fledge 126 baby martins in our various nests.

4:12 p.m.—UPS came to pick up our finished orders. We shipped a total of 319 pounds of rope to four different states. A number of other orders were worked on but not finished.

5:10 p.m.—Amanda and Mary were still in the shop when we had a call from one of our regular customers in Iowa, who ordered 70 spools (42,000 feet). Earlier we got a four-spool order from Texas.

Sherry Pardee

FOR THE BIRDS. Dried gourds from the garden will make mighty fine martin houses.

5:15 p.m.—For supper we had baked chicken and potatoes, peas and carrots and coleslaw.

Outdoors it started to rain, but the wood stove kept us very cozy around the supper table, where we exchanged the day's happenings at school and at home.

We talked about how we should be thankful to no end for a happy Christian home, a warm and dry house and such good food.

Dessert was blueberry cheese pie and Adams County apple cake, both from recipes in *Country* magazine. We added just a bit of ice cream, and I need not to tell you more.

Before leaving the table our family circle sang *I Thank My God.*

7:30 p.m.—I finished reading those circle letters while the children played a few games.

8:45 p.m.—The children got ready for bed. Momma got Marcus ready, too. He wasn't feeling his best because of a cold. She fixed him a bottle of juice, sang a song for him and rocked him as he softly drifted away to sleep. What a blessing to be able to provide for our dear family!

9 p.m.— We showered and then hit the sack. We were very tired, but still thanked God for all our blessings. Good night.

His Day's Work at Sawmill Is Satisfying

◆ PROFILE ◆

Norman and Lori Ann Miller are just getting started with dairying and raising beef cattle on their 100-acre farm near Mio. Hay is their main crop. Norman also is a partner in a three-man sawmill. The Millers have a daughter, Dorothy, 2. Norman kept this diary.

Whoo-oo! Whoo-oo! Chug! Chug! Clangety-clang-clang! The faithful old train alarm jars us fully awake before it completes its second circuit around the track. Its bright, perky little face informs us it's 5 a.m., time to get up and at it!

I roll out, and by the time I've got the fires stirred up and the lanterns hissing brightly, Lori is preparing my lunch and getting breakfast started. It's 43° outside and not snowing like it was 24 hours ago.

5:30: I head for the barn to feed the 10 calves we've got; we're aiming to have 30 or more before winter. By 6 I'm back inside and washed up.

Lori has Dorothy up and dressed, and breakfast is on the table, consisting of eggs, toast and corn flakes.

6:35: Breakfast and devotions over, I head across the lawn to stoke the fire at our parochial schoolhouse before continuing to work.

It's raining some, so Lori plans to do some canning today instead of washing clothes as she would normally. She's got the last of the tomatoes to do and some grapes, too.

TWO-WHEELED "STEED". Short trip to sawmill means there's no need to hitch horse.

7 a.m.: At the mill, we've finished our daily preparations (sharpening saw bits and warming up engines). The sawmill roars to life with the acceleration of our three power units, which run the "Meadow Mill" headsaw, "Min-

REGULAR ROUTE. Before heading to the sawmill (below), Norman feeds calves in the barn (right) and stokes the fire at nearby schoolhouse (above).

er" edger and "Morbark" chipper.

The diesel lift truck is already purring for another day, and it's time to start the diesel unit on our "Barko" clam loader, which we use to keep our live deck (log skidway) loaded.

This business is owned jointly by my dad, brother-in-law and myself. We produce strictly pine landscape timbers, which are pressure-treated after being sold to lumber companies. Our waste wood is chipped and hauled to power plants to generate electricity.

This morning finds brother Lester on the headsaw, brother-in-law Dennis edging and stacking and me doing routine bookwork, cleaning up and keeping bundles banded and moved.

8:30: Some children pedal past on their way to school, and soon another bicycle and then a buggy follow.

9:15: Coffee break! Working the sawmill is fairly strenuous, and I'm glad for the overstuffed lunch bucket, thanks to my industrious wife. I quickly eat some popcorn and ice cream and drink a cup of coffee. By 9:30 we're back at work.

This shift finds me on the headsaw, Lester railsawing and Dennis trimming the bundles down to 96 inches. By changing off like this, the day seems to go faster.

11:45: Lunchtime. Skies have cleared up and the sun is shining brightly, proof once more that weather can change fast in Michigan.

I take a peek up toward the farm but don't see any wash flapping in the breeze. Evidently Lori is sticking to her plans.

12:30: Back to the daily roar. Dennis is tailsawing, and I'm still dicing logs. Lester goes for a dentist appointment, leaving us a little short-handed.

2:15: Last coffee break for today, and by 2:30 we're on our last shift, with Dennis on the saw and the stacking falling on my shoulders.

3:15: Scholars are leaving for home now, but it's too far out to the road to wave to them. One of the live deck chains derails, resulting in an old-fashioned log jam.

We keep going until 4, then do this 'n' that that needs to be done before tomorrow. Today's tally comes to only 8,000 board feet. Generally we get around 12,000 board feet.

5 o'clock finds me at home once more. Lori has the countertop filled with her day's accomplishments—30 quarts of grape juice, 13 pints of pizza sauce and 7 pints of beet jelly (yum!). This, plus her "daily dozens" kept her busy today, and she's still cleaning up when I head for the barn to get the feeding and chores done.

5:45: I grab my bow and arrows and take off for my tree stand, hoping a deer will come through tonight.

We normally eat supper at 6, but we'll wait tonight until I get back.

7:45: Too dark to shoot. I head for the house nearly half a mile across the fields. No deer in sight, though Lester informs me at the house that he saw a buck and several does down at the sawmill. Oh, well!

8:30: Supper is past, and Lori's finishing the dishes while I look at the mail and play with Dorothy.

9:30: We make preparations for bed, and after commending our bodies and souls in God's almighty hands, we hit the sack.

The impudent little "Whoo-oo, Whoo-oo" alarm gets set for another morning. A look at its eager little face shows 10 minutes after 10. In several minutes, all's quiet at the Millers'.

With Lots of Lunches, Loaves Don't Last

◆ PROFILE ◆

Allen and Esther Miller milk six cows, feed a few pigs and grow corn, oats and hay on their 110-acre farm near Millesrburg, Ohio. Several family members work at a local bakery, and Allen repairs farm machinery. The Millers have 11 children: Mary, 22, Ervin, 21, Wayne, 19, Andy, 17, Leona, 16, Marvin, 15, William, 12, Ada, 11, Elizabeth, 9, Aaron, 7, and Laura, 6. Esther kept this diary.

The alarm went off at 5:30. With a peek out the window at the clear sky with the moon brightly shining, how can one not help breathing a prayer of thankfulness to the God who watches over us?

Soon I was in the kitchen with lunch buckets to pack while Allen and the boys went to the barn to do the chores and milking. There are six cows to milk, four work horses, three road horses and a few pigs to feed. Marvin also has a few rabbits.

The girls got up to help with the buckets; we have nine to pack, which is not bad if I'm prepared!

After a breakfast of eggs and toast, oatmeal, cinnamon rolls and hot tea, Ervin was first to leave. He is a mechanic at Semac Industries.

Mary left shortly after for Fryburg Parochial School, where she is teaching her second term. With 27 pupils, her days are always busy ones. She goes the 3-mile trek from here with horse-and-buggy.

Wayne and Andy left soon after. Wayne works for Berlin Paints and Solvents, mixing stain for wood shops all over Ohio. Andy works at Milwood Products at Bunker Hill, making lawn furniture and crafts.

The girls' leaving for school will pretty well take care of the lunch buckets. They had egg sandwiches with slices of tomatoes to put on, also pear salad, which somehow survived the weekend, plus cookies and pretzels.

Counting sandwiches, we used 17 slices of bread for all the lunch buckets. Some days the boys will choose to have leftover casseroles or soup instead of sandwiches.

The chores being done in the barn, the rest of the family also had breakfast. Ada and Elizabeth did the dishes while I helped the two youngest comb their hair and get their coats on.

The five scholars left a little after 8 to join some more of the neighbor children on their way. They don't have far to go, around 1/4-mile to the one-room school, Scenic View, on top of the hill. On occasion they come home at noon to eat, like last week when we filled silo—they knew there would be plenty of their favorite foods.

> *"Before getting the wash in I took a 10-minute snooze..."*

Leona had gathered the hampers of wash before breakfast and took them to the basement, so I did the washing. With 14 loads to be done, it took most of the morning. The lines were full, so I had to take some off before I could hang the rest of it up.

What a nice wash day again! Because it was a bit windy, one of the lines tore down, but the wash was dry, so I brought it in. We wash on Mondays, Wednesdays and Fridays, so we appreciate nice wash days.

Leona had a dress to finish before going to work at 10 at Homestead Restaurant in Charm. Marvin went squirrel hunting. A neighbor came by with a feed grinder to have it repaired, so Allen welded it for him.

At noon we had vegetable soup that we canned this fall, plus Swiss cheese and tomato sandwiches and Jell-O. Later, Allen's sister Emma stopped in for a chat as she went after the mail.

Emma lives in Grandpa Daudy's house with her sister Sara and Daudy (Allen's dad), who is 83 years old. She keeps house for him and his widowed sister, Lizzie, who is 89. Daudy is outside every day and tinkers around in his shop.

Before getting in more of the wash, I took a 10-minute snooze. Then I cleaned Allen's Sunday suit. Our church district had Communion yesterday at neighbor Roy Miller's. Yesterday it was 17 years ago that Allen was ordained deacon in our church.

This afternoon Marvin helped me cut grapes. We got three dishpans full but didn't quite get them all, as there is a yellow jacket nest in the walls of the woodhouse, and we stayed a fair distance from that.

When the scholars came home, Aaron and his buddy Robert found a nice shady spot under the maple tree to eat their leftover snack from their buckets until the other children caught up with them.

Laura washed the school buckets, and Ada got in the rest of the wash and put it away. There are always dozens of stockings and socks to sort and fold. Then they helped Aaron pick up apples in the orchard. We will use some of them to make cider with the small press we have here.

For supper we had mashed potatoes and gravy, meat loaf, corn, applesauce, then ice cream, as William's 13th birthday will be tomorrow. Ervin worked late, so we held supper for him.

DAD brought home lots of beef tallow from Baltic Meats, which we rendered for lye soap. I made two big batches, using 10 cans of lye for one and 8 cans for the other. Mixed each batch in a big iron kettle, wearing rubber gloves.

I rubbed the crumbly soap through a 1/4-inch mesh screen, then poured it on old bed sheets to dry for 10 days or so. It was shared with several of the children—makes very nice laundry soap. *—Mary Ann Miller, Baltic, Ohio*